For # Mirkey

Let hope

quote you

always!

Love,

[signature]

these are the pages

For the Good of the Party
or
The Range of Acceptable Dosages

Hart L'Ecuyer

For all the poets
lost & forgotten
to time

"Come, wander with me," she said,
"Into regions yet untrod;
And read what is still unread
In the manuscripts of God."

Henry Wadsworth Longfellow

FOR THE GOOD OF THE PARTY

building's metal bones
malleable is the heart
bends only for you

roadside sunflower
did somebody plant you there?
I think they must have

light catches a face
it's not the time for curtains
she sees me staring

I bought a coffee
how much time does that buy me?
don't wanna go home

there are some free things
but love isn't one of them
let me pay for this

what is your refrain?
what will be carved on your grave?
think on your last words

under construction
improvements are coming soon
for now, be careful

the Arctic's melting
Jesus Christ humanity
what a mess you've made

Church is in trouble
millions of hymnals are closed
one song is drowned out

Donald Trump said this
Kim Kardashian wore that
Hart L'Ecuyer quiet

a red sun rises
over a small parking lot
out in the suburbs

cocaine keeps me up
I don't usually see dawn
the grass needs mowing

blowing my poor nose
crowd gone, beer cans everywhere
excellent party

the moth of August
flies on the edge of your sight
incandescent night

the straight & narrow
does not inspire description
let's run in circles

"light a cigarette"
commands pack of cigarettes
barefoot, sleepless: "yes"

calligraphic clouds
DARPA done us right today
I'm only joking

too many blossoms
not near enough parking lots
tryna keep it real

magazines litter
expensive coffee table
above, fan blade turns

homeless man picks up
cigarette butt from the ground
I offer him one

you only notice
sound of the highway at night
where are they going?

blades of grass rustle
green leaves on the trees rustle
wind opens my book

sound of cicadas
the lack of her touching me
porch light reaches out

I gulp down a beer
for the good of the party
who's got a lighter?

way up in the sky
someone walks to the bathroom
I do the same here

quicker than music
but slower than headlights
oh goodness! it's you

at dusk the city
sinks into an August night
dirty from the day

NOCTURNES & AUBADES

Begun 4 November 2018
Completed 13 November 2018

The Bones of Nocturne

the bones of
nocturne the sum
total of the
fight between jumping
to religious conclusions & seeing
songs picking
them up in your
hand then dropping
them on
the floor having
been shown poverty

the bones of nocturne the
orgasmic manna calling
out to a lazily
naked lover putting
on airs &
pants & panting
from the effort building
muscle where
necessary someone
has to

the bones
of nocturne entering
the bedroom for sleep &
vines creep like rodents onto
the house which
is infested with
rats which you can
hear even in your
drunken stupor scratching
in the walls

the
bones of nocturne video
game insomnia spinning
out a Corvette unshaven &
smelling like
death & then going
for a walk in
the fog because
your cat doesn't
need to get high

the bones of
nocturne the numbness on
your lips from the
cocaine which you
got for free from
a friend who is also
an enemy but still you
drink his beer you
worry it will
come out

the bones of nocturne the
donation of blood leaving
you in a tube lucky
for some other
person wearing
a purse as a man because
you like the color &
the roominess you
sling it over your
shoulder

the bones
of nocturne the pattern
of behavior that keeps
you coming back for
less & less connection to
the world there is
so much laundry piled
up to do & so many
things to vote on
next week

the
bones of nocturne
are yes
my bones gulping
wine at every
opportunity setting
sail for dreams any
minute now anxiously
wondering how random
things are manufactured

the bones of
nocturne manifest
themselves as shaking
hands with my fellow
Americans that is the
secret blue flame
sinfully severed from
the gas line of
possibility but we
want what we want

the bones of nocturne the
grasping at
laws made by the deep
waters in the mind that
place everyone can
dive into perhaps to
hunt for treasure or
to bathe in the
unconscious hurricane

the bones
of nocturne no
longer restless a
moth flies around
the lamp he
always turns on before turning
in his identification at
the gate of the
city where he is
destined to die

Rainy Aubade

rainy aubade
aubade for my name
playing with my hair aubade
getting old fast aubade
aubade for car accidents
day drinking aubade
historical events aubade
going to the movies aubade
aubade for the city of lights
muddy aubade
getting mad over nothing aubade
radicalization of the far ends of the political spectrum aubade
bending over to pick up something you dropped aubade
coffeeshop aubade
aubade for the rain stopping

Autumnal Aubade

fall colors aubade
autumnal aubade
yellow & red & orange aubade
aubade for gray sky
getting work done aubade
wearing jackets aubade
vaping aubade
quitting cigarettes aubade
aubade for health
aubade for new romance
aubade for school
aubade for following along
going to church aubade
going to the hardware store aubade
missing someone who's gone aubade
visiting their grave aubade
saying words to them even though they can't hear aubade
aubade for the dead
aubade for the dying
weddings & funerals aubade
aubade for it all being a part of the same process aubade
aubade for strip malls
fancy cars aubade
autumnal aubade

Aubade on Aubades

oh now you're just listing things aubade
oh I see how it is aubade
just things that come into your head aubade
metapoetic aubade
aubade for people who don't like aubades normally
these are the aubades
late afternoon now aubade
not even an aubade anymore aubade
getting almost time for a nocturne aubade
what even is an aubade
of aubades, by aubades, for aubades
god bless America aubade
mow the grass aubade
have sex aubade
listen to some music aubade
I see what you're doing now aubade

Aubade from Pastiche of Dylan Thomas

slice of bread aubade
killing two birds with one stone aubade
getting pretty wordy now aubade
aubade go die
aubade on the top of a hill
listening to church bells aubade
climbing a tree long ago aubade
indulging in something joyful aubade
having a heart attack aubade
getting buried alive aubade
looting a city aubade
alternatively phrased, searching for supplies aubade
hurricanes aubade
scaly aubade
cloak & dagger aubade
aubade for angels
aubade for demons
aubade for cupped hands
aubade for clocks that don't work anymore but you still keep them
aubade for flowing
aubade for knowing
that tomorrow is coming soon you
know what that
means:
nocturnes, baby!

Aubade for the Coming Nocturnes

in a few hours after
dinner the aubades will be
over & it will be
time for nocturnes again aubade
reading Ecclesiastes aubade
reading Allen Ginsberg aubade
aubade for skimming
aubade for skinnydipping
aubade for doing acid
getting way too high aubade
going the wrong way on a one-way street aubade
getting
ready to write some nocturnes aubade
getting
fucked up aubade
getting
a handjob in a boat aubade
getting gotten aubade
getting into some trouble aubade
aubade for that
hombreezo aubade
streetcutter aubade
transgender aubade
identity politics aubade
divisiveness aubade
coming together over tragedy rq aubade
aubade for America
maybe we'll do that next
yeah let's do that next

Aubade for America

aubade for America
aubade for Americans
aubade for Obama
aubade for Trump
Hillary Clinton aubade
Bernie Sanders aubade
Gary Johnson aubade
farmland aubade
bars that take sides aubades
elections that result in divorces aubade
elections that lose you friends aubade
going to the hospital & paying way too much aubade
broken healthcare system aubade
military industrial complex aubade
school to prison pipeline aubade
skyscraper aubade
entrepreneur aubade
aubade for rich people
aubade for poor people
aubade for the vanishing middle class
god bless America aubade

Jordan Peterson Aubade

denouncing humanity itself aubade
homecoming queen aubade
owning a dog aubade
a serious error has been made aubade
aubade for men being dangerous
aubade for remembering the old joke
aubade for something to think about aubade
have you taken full advantage aubade
proving troublesome aubade
the phrase "sex life" aubade
subscribing to a theory aubade
aubade for boys being boys
aubade for boys not being boys
girls being girls aubade
girls being boys aubade
by the early 1940's aubade
living in Boston aubade
making a bad decision aubade
having the time of your life aubade
what, then, do you stand against? aubade
turning thirteen years old aubade
aubade for victory
aubade for Orwell quotes
aubade for having a small nose
famous aubade
maybe more like infamous aubade
Jordan Peterson aubade

Allen Ginsberg Aubade

aubade in a desert oasis aubade
the wit the courage & the faith aubade
breathing slowly aubade
wanting someone's approval aubade
causing someone to grieve aubade
going out for ice cream aubade
big headed aubade
bracelet aubade

Bomb Aubade

bombing run aubade
aubade for the people who make the bombs
aubade for the people that die from the bombs
aubade for the people that profit from the bombs
aubade for the people that vote for the bombs
aubade for the people that don't vote at all aubade
voter registration drive aubade
Claire McCaskill aubade
right to work wrong for Missouri aubade

Allen Ginsberg Aubade Part II

halo aubade
not this time aubade
big mouth aubade
portal to another world aubade
beating heart aubade
tongue in cheek aubade
surprising aubade
forgiveness aubade

Kesha Aubade

sick beat aubade
rehabilitated aubade
obsession aubade
desperate calls aubade
what you got boy is hard to find aubade
strung out aubade
your love is my drug aubade
crackhead aubade
can't get you off my mind aubade

Allen Ginsberg Aubade Part III

glitter bomb aubade
already talked about bombs but not this kind of bomb aubade
aubade for skulls
aubade for ossuaries
aubade for the English crown
it's all perspective aubade
chemistry aubade
sad face aubade
American flag aubade

International Aubade

Tanzania aubade
Monaco aubade
Russia aubade
all the countries aubade
Congo Canada Japan aubade
things you can't get in America aubade
I went on a Caribbean cruise once aubade
I've performed in Berlin, Prague, Zurich, & Paris aubade
want to see more of it aubade
Mexico aubade
made in China aubade
YKK zipper aubade
Portuguese-speaking countries aubade
Francophone countries aubade
aubade for Europe aubade for Asia

Aubade Against the President

aubade for globalism
aubade for xenophobes
aubade for white supremacist in White House
aubade for embarrassing the nation on the world stage
aubade for sending soldiers to kill refugees of disastrous foreign policy aubade
bad ideas that are shockingly popular aubade
populism aubade
barely won the election aubade
should have been Bernie Sanders aubade
aubade for hate
aubade for Proud Boys
aubade for Nazis
aubade for Republicans
aubade for textbook toxic masculinity
aubade for "demoncrats"
aubade for "feminism is cancer"
aubade for white male violence
aubade for white male guns
aubade against white male supremacy
aubade against the "president"

Allen Ginsberg Aubade Part IV

muscular aubade
Nashville aubade
green aubade
aubade for hardons
70 mph aubade
drums aubade
endlessness aubade

Pessimism Aubade

existentialist aubade
nihilist aubade
zero sum game aubade
nothing to lose nothing to win aubade
depression aubade

Crepuscular Aubade

it's almost time for a nocturne aubade
this is one of the last aubades of the day aubade
crepuscular aubade
twilight aubade
dinnertime aubade

Dancing Aubade

leaving one's head & heart on the dance floor aubade
listening to Lady Gaga aubade
lose your mind aubade
make a request of the DJ aubade
out at the club aubade
this isn't Chicago aubade

Allen Ginsberg Aubade Part V

19th century aubade
toward the door aubade
aubade for being of one mind
aubade for factions
aubade for the Ozarks
aubade for the random shit Allen Ginsberg wrote about over the years aubade

The Final Aubade of the Day

laughing it off aubade
dusting off your trousers aubade
floating aubade
happy aubade
nickel & dime aubade
amusement park aubade
don't give out on me yet aubade
aubade for the end of 4 November 2018
aubade for that
yeah

The Eyes of Nocturne

the eyes of
nocturne the curtains are
open the floors need
someone to fall down
crying because of what
isn't true but you wish it
was there's nothing
inside it is an empty
crystal decanter which
should be full

the eyes of nocturne the
table where it is writing the
nocturne the seeing how
things far away can
have bearing on
us bearing
down on us looking
down on us it is too
early to get cozy & too
late for other things

the eyes
of nocturne on the
mantel is a clock in the
clock are gears gears
don't contain anything it
doesn't feel like it does
either you
live the life you've
imagined or you die the
death you deserve

the
eyes of nocturne fall
upon itself & its
wine glass which is nearly
need of filling which
costs money like most
things

The Abandonment Nocturne

I have changed
my mind the
pattern was good for
last night but this nocturne
is the nocturne
of abandonment
of leaving behind
of forging new
trails nocturne
hitting up friends to hang out nocturne
nothing to do on Sunday 4 November nocturne
election day approaches nocturne
time to get serious with these nocturnes

Uncle Bill's Nocturne

just coffee for this nocturne
the Uncle Bill's Pancake House nocturne
the nocturne of listening in on conversations
this nocturne isn't going anywhere for a WHILE
this nocturne comes with ketchup & isn't
crowded I might get
some food later we'll
see

Nocturne of the Unused Knife

I can see how it
might seem like this
nocturne isn't saying
anything the truth couldn't
be scarier it's
true I could tell
you the wifi code or
the menu or what
the two other
parties are talking
about but I think
for this nocturne we'll
just soak it
in

Nocturne Prominently Featuring Bacon

strawberry shortcake nocturne
fish dinner nocturne
blueberry pancakes nocturne
slice of toast nocturne
nocturne prominently featuring bacon

Fork & Spoon Nocturne

fork &
spoon nocturne staring at
the eaves nocturne
nobody to kick it with nocturne
lonely nocturne
nocturne of the pushed aside
silverware

Peace-Loving Nocturne

these nocturnes are just warming up nocturne
I'll take some more nocturne
I'm only nocturne
I have nothing to nocturne
trusting in nocturne
safe & warm in nocturne
all's well in this nocturne
no war touches this nocturne
this is a non-violent nocturne
a peace-loving nocturne

The Flesh of Nocturne

the flesh of
nocturne the
threshing of a nocturne
the net's meshing
of nocturne
fishers of men nocturne
don't talk to me about god nocturne
bread & butter nocturne
softball nocturne
easy to comprehend nocturne

the flesh of nocturne the
new world order of
nocturne Obamas & Clintons yo
mamas & Clintons Osamas & Clintons
can't seem to ever
get rid of these
Clintons a
nocturne for that nocturne for the CIA
a nocturne for Jesus

the flesh
of nocturne teach
me to nocturne reach
out to me with a nocturne
banish me to a nocturne
adore the nocturne
make more nocturnes

We Dem Nocturnes

ay
nocturnes
hola, hola
hola, we dem nocturnes
hola, hola, hola
we our lips burn
we taking left turns
hola, we dem nocturnes
hola, hola, hola
grab a menu
smell of fatty pancakes they gone come
asked her out uh-oh cause she only say Um
hola, hola, hola
we dem nocturnes

Joke Nocturne

two nocturnes
walk into a bar
one of the nocturnes
orders a gin & tonic
the other nocturne
doesn't have any money so he
just sits there drinking water until
someone takes pity on him
& buys him a
beer

Big Screen Nocturne

I'm gonna make a
movie about my
nocturnes & all the
parts will be
played by real
live nocturnes like
this one & people will
gobble popcorn during the
film which will be a
documentary about how
great my nocturnes are

Trumpy Nocturne

these nocturnes are the
best nocturnes they're
the biggest nocturnes there
are folks nobody
has bigger
nocturnes folks
we are gonna
make nocturnes
great again!

Contagious Nocturnes

contagious nocturnes
pages of nocturnes
buckets of nocturne
little vials of nocturne
block-long warehouses full of nocturnes
nocturne factories
nocturne neighborhoods where only
nocturnes live
subterranean nocturnes
skyscraper nocturnes
town nocturnes county nocturnes
male nocturnes female nocturnes
big nocturnes small nocturnes
gay & straight nocturnes
Pakistani nocturnes
Hindu nocturnes
attractive nocturnes
oriental nocturnes
politically correct nocturnes
needle nocturnes
nights out late nocturnes
long road nocturnes

Burn All the Nocturnes

burn all the
nocturnes kill off
nocturnes breed more
nocturnes in a nocturne
mill mama nocturnes daddy nocturnes
baby sister nocturnes
baby brother nocturnes
I am the nocturnes

Usurping Nocturnes

extrajudicial nocturnes
outdoor nocturnes
significant nocturnes
footnote to nocturnes
breathless & sticky nocturnes
unruly & rebellious nocturnes
usurping nocturnes
nocturnes upon nocturnes
the bodies of nocturnes
burial of nocturne
funereal nocturne
nocturnes that don't take no for an answer
political nocturnes
Christmas nocturnes
hole in the wall nocturnes
mapping out my soul with nocturnes
crazy nocturnes
lazy nocturnes
cool nocturnes
nocturnes that are going places
the evolution of nocturnes
associating with nocturnes
conglomerate nocturnes
nocturnes that don't
know their place
teenage nocturnes
nocturne "riots"
usurping nocturnes
not gonna
take it anymore nocturnes
revolutionary nocturnes
Turquoise nocturnes
red & blue nocturnes
donkey, elephant, & giraffe nocturnes
safari nocturne
nocturne poachers

Yummy Nocturnes

roast nocturne
nocturne edibles
smokable nocturne
delicious nocturnes
nocturnes you can only get here
nocturnes with hot sauce
jello nocturnes
salted & peppered nocturnes

Interior of a Nocturne

overhead lights nocturne
carpeting nocturne
burst of energy nocturne
scene kid nocturne
addiction to nocturne
technicolor nocturne
dictionary of the nocturne language

Sexy Nocturne

hairy nocturne
nocturne between her legs
kissing her nocturnes
rubbing her nocturnes
getting my nocturnes off
splattering nocturne on a picture of Grandma
waking up her entire nocturne with all the
noise
she
makes
making
more nocturnes
out of breath
have a cigarette

Nocturne Without a Theme

dingy nocturne
nocturne without a theme
falling onto my hands & knees nocturne
American nocturne
fatuous nocturne
nocturne born of cocaine
conceived in coffee

Expletive Nocturne

fuck the nocturne!
down with nocturnes!
no nocturne, no peace!
pulling the plug on a nocturne
decorating your nocturne

Nocturne God

godless nocturnes
Catholic nocturnes
faithful, faithless, & Masonic nocturnes
better than no nocturnes at all
ancient as the Knights Templar nocturne
cave wall nocturne
temple nocturne
church & mosque & synagogue nocturne
mass shooter nocturne
contemporary nocturnes
prostrate nocturnes
conmen nocturnes
hateful nocturnes
theoretical nocturnes
ever-changing nocturnes

Flux Nocturne

flux nocturne
one moment it's a nocturne
& the next it's a
clownhead
linear nocturnes
exponential nocturnes
mathematically impossible nocturnes
charted nocturnes
plotted-out nocturnes

Guy Fawkes Nocturne

plotting nocturnes
scheming nocturnes
Guy Fawkes 5th of November nocturne
July 4th nocturne
September 11th nocturne
December 7th nocturne
Elba was a nocturne
think Napoleon didn't know about nocturnes?
think again
my coffee cup a nocturne
your genitals a nocturne
the nearest full-size chandelier a nocturne
nocturnes in hindsight
nocturnes brought to you by
Wells Fargo

Nostalgic Nocturnes

rosy-cheeked nocturne
checkered picnic nocturne
French braids nocturne
music you used to like nocturne
the nocturne of your first time

Death Nocturne

the nocturne of your last time
nocturne of the hour
Hail Mary nocturne
fork over all your nocturnes!
robbed at gunpoint nocturne
brush with death nocturne

Heroin Nocturne

overdose nocturne
nocturne for my drug dealers
a nocturne for the users
a nocturne for the abusers
Narcotics Anonymous nocturne
candlelight vigil nocturne

Joseph Suh's Nocturne

here is a
nocturne for
Joe
who
hanged himself
he was
my
roommate
I felt
partially responsible
I bullied him
I had never
been popular before

Chicago Nocturne

Chicago nocturne
viaduct nocturne
cigarette nocturne
nocturne for mania
Armadillo's Pillow nocturne
Loyola University nocturne
Lake Michigan sex nocturne
alcohol poisoning nocturne
unprotected sex nocturne
seriously I'm not possessed Joe nocturne
two kids that couldn't
have been more different
nocturne

Gray Nocturne

atheist nocturne
gravel nocturne
Babylon nocturne
stone wall nocturne
civil war nocturne
nocturne for nocturne
nocturne against nocturnes

The Sermon on the Nocturne

blessed be the nocturnes
for they will inherit the earth

John's Gospel Nocturne

in the beginning
was the nocturne
& the nocturne was with
god
& the nocturne was
god
the same was in the beginning with
god
all nocturnes
came to be through him
& without him was not any
nocturne
made
that was
made
& the nocturne shineth in the darkness
& the darkness
has not
overcome it

Pink Nocturne

frilly nocturne
pirated nocturne
nocturne & chill
sugary nocturne
bitch nocturne
oops nocturne

Landmark Nocturnes

nocturne fart
nocturne the vinyl record
musical nocturne
blaring nocturne
nocturnes you can see for miles
big nocturnes
nocturne tombs
nocturne pyramids
souvenir nocturnes
exit through the nocturne gift shop

Blue Nocturnes

oceanic nocturne
nocturne beaches
honeymoon nocturnes
nocturne rain

Nocturnes That Are Only Nocturnes

nocturne republic
nocturne monarchy
fading nocturnes
nocturnes that can't be compared to other things
nocturnes that are only nocturnes

Music Nocturnes

harmonica nocturne
nocturne flutes
entire symphony nocturne

Sadface Nocturne

bittersweet nocturnes
nocturne breakups
nocturne industrial complex
raptured nocturnes
apocalypse nocturne
bloody nocturne
warring frowning just plain bad nocturnes

Bookish Nocturnes

straightforward nocturnes
nocturnes that mind their own business
English nocturnes
nocturne prudes
nocturne scholars
books on the subject of nocturnes

Thinking Outside the Nocturne

maybe that's
enough nocturnes for
now? that sure is
a lot of nocturnes
let's think outside
the nocturne here

The Girl in the Nocturne

go-getter nocturne
nocturnes on bikes
nocturne boobs
vaginal nocturne
blue jeans-wearing nocturnes
yoga-doing nocturnes
nocturnes sunbathing in Tower Grove Park
ambitious nocturnes
vegetarian nocturnes

Suburban Nocturne

in the suburbs I
wrote nocturnes
& they told me my
nocturnes
would never
survive
you always seemed so sure
that one day we'd
write nocturnes

In the Nocturnes I

in the nocturnes I
live, eat, shit, breathe, fuck, love, hate
in the
nocturnes I
wade up to my
knees
I find myself
not being
able to
believe

It Meant Nothing

these nocturnes
have no
poignant statement to refract the complexities of post-modern life
nor are they symbols

The Crossed-Out Nocturnes

I have
crossed out
several
nocturnes
they shall
not
be
remembered
(RIP)

Nature vs. Nocturne

nature
versus
nocturne:
who would win?

Pain: A Nocturne

pains me a nocturne
like a rock in my shoe
pain is
everywhere
like nocturnes
the difference is
that you
write nocturnes
& pain
writes you

Symmetrical Nocturnes

symmetrical nocturnes
laconic nocturnes
corporate nocturnes
thirteen thousand ways of looking at a nocturne
Jerusalem nocturne
brand name nocturne
fractal nocturne
20/20 nocturne
virgin nocturne
linebacker nocturne
sup nocturne
sacrilegious nocturne
pumpkin spice nocturne
nocturne alarm
Ozymandias nocturne
microscopic nocturnes
collectible nocturnes
Jason Bourne nocturne
godzilla nocturne
copyrighting happy birthday nocturne
should have thought of that myself nocturne
nocturne in the nude
cocksure nocturne
nocturne empties
sacristy nocturne
Molotov nocturne
mind the gap between nocturnes
getting lost in nocturnes
capricious nocturnes

Terrifying Nocturnes

terrifying nocturnes
nocturnes with a thousand eyes
horned nocturnes
nocturnes that are monsters
the nocturnes they talk about around campfires
nocturnes that can kill
nocturnes that do kill
vengeful nocturnes
jealous nocturnes

Beautiful Nocturnes

beautiful nocturnes
nocturnes of angels
nocturnes worthy only of heaven
nocturnes that cannot be relayed here

Secret Nocturnes

secret nocturnes
Masonic nocturnes
nocturnes older than Rome
nocturnes which I am privy to
nocturnes which I am not privy to
Vatican nocturnes
Swiss bank vault nocturnes
Nazi bunker nocturnes
alien nocturnes
Mayan nocturnes
Egyptian nocturnes
nocturnes in code

Coded Nocturne

20-8-9-19_9-19_1_3-15-4-5-4_14-15-3-20-21-18-14-5
if I had any crucial to say I would have said it here

Narrative Nocturne

eventful nocturne
nocturnes that tell stories
epic nocturnes
a nocturne about a hero
a villainous nocturne
a noble nocturne
a nocturne to remember
a nocturne to dissect

Nocturne for MFA Programs

nocturne not found

Robotic Nocturne

hello my name is Nocturne
how can I assist you today?

Party Nocturne

vomiting nocturne
holding her hair back nocturne
snorting cocaine off her best china nocturne
going back to her place nocturne
fucking her twice each time just as bad nocturne
waking up in the morning to write aubades nocturne

Mystery Box Nocturne

you never know what you're gonna get with nocturnes
brain damage from football nocturne
she blows you a kiss nocturne
wishing you hadn't given away your coat nocturne
charity that you regret later nocturne

Virtuous Nocturne

noble nocturne
chaste nocturne
nocturne with a lot of integrity
brave nocturne
patriotic nocturne

Soldier Nocturne

battle armor nocturne
marching boots nocturne
automatic rifle nocturne
emergency nocturne provisions
nocturne in your sights

Nocturne Targets

enemy nocturne
brown nocturne
Muslim nocturne
innocent nocturne
nocturne who's only a child
hospital nocturne
newspaper nocturne
wedding in Yemen nocturne

Wedding Nocturne

wedding nocturne
nocturne of love
binding nocturne
nocturne toasts
nocturne cake
saying hi to everybody nocturne
thank you for coming such a long way nocturne
you may now kiss the nocturne

Unreal City Nocturne

city of nocturnes
unreal nocturne
teeming with nocturnes
nocturnes with turned-up collars
bowler hat nocturnes
briefcase & overcoat nocturnes
business nocturnes

Random Nocturnes

bridge between nocturne A & nocturne B
expensive nocturne
diamond nocturne
royalty nocturne
nocturne I can't read because my handwriting is illegible
a stubborn pattern emerges in the nocturne

Trout Fishing in America Nocturne

Dear Trout Fishing in America Nocturne,
it's very late at
night & I am
not sleeping what are
you up to?
Love,
Hart

Inter-Galactic Nocturne

inter-galactic nocturne
spaceship nocturne
tractor beam nocturne
nocturnes that span galaxies
nocturnes that travel at the speed of light
nocturnes that can't be contained

Outlaw Nocturne

outlaw nocturne
heretical nocturne
nocturne that'll get me burned at the stake
frontier nocturne
wild wild west nocturne
Ace high nocturne

Asymmetrical Nocturne

a real mess of a nocturne
a nocturne that needs a good haircut
the kind of nocturne your mother warned you about
the kind of nocturne that couldn't be an aubade
all over the place nocturne
manic depressive but mostly manic nocturne
period blood on bedsheets nocturne
mud caked on the stairs nocturne
haven't showered in four days nocturne

Indecipherable Nocturne

Navajo nocturne
handwritten nocturne
babbling nocturne
cursive nocturne
nocturne that coincides with a cinematic explosion

Fiery Nocturnes

fiery nocturnes
pyromaniac nocturnes
fabric fireproofing spray nocturnes
nocturne fireworks
4th of July nocturnes
arson nocturnes
passionate nocturnes

Masturbatory Nocturne

masturbatory nocturne
self-indulgent nocturne
right-handed nocturne
thinking of you nocturne
hard cock nocturne

Moire Nocturnes

latticework of nocturnes
nocturne trestles
braided nocturnes
flyover nocturnes
moire nocturnes

<u>Nocturne for Jess Adkins</u>

you are not the
girl with blue
hair but I
do quite
like you this
could also be called
the philosopher's nocturne
a questioning nocturne
a seeker after nocturne
a nocturne I remember lying in a hammock with once
wasn't that nice?

Nocturne as Necktie

red power nocturne
blue & white striped nocturne
purple paisley nocturne
checkered nocturne
skinny brown nocturne
nocturne with little billikens on it
aquatic nocturne

Deep Sea Nocturne

deep sea nocturne
scuba nocturne
coral reef nocturne
global warming nocturne
Al Gore nocturne
tricky issue nocturne
whale nocturne
save the whales!

Event Nocturnes

natural disaster nocturne
Halloween party nocturne
Tchaikovsky nocturne
presidential inauguration nocturne
birth of your firstborn nocturne
death of your father nocturne
wedding nocturne
arrival of the pope in your hometown nocturne
prize fight nocturne

This Day in History Aubade

by far the most interesting thing
that happened on this aubade in history
is Guy Fawkes who
was in charge of the
explosives but there were a number of
other plotters involved in the aubade

Allen Ginsberg Aubade Part VI

psychiatric aubade
endless aubade
daisy aubade
itching aubade
four billion years aubade

Unwritten Aubade

one of the aubades
isn't written down
it
just floats there
not being
known
or
understood I
think if I
was an aubade I would
want to be
written down but hey

Aubade in a Cage

aubade in a cage
aubade with claws
aubade in a circus
freak show aubade
aubade you gotta pay money to see
special exhibit aubade

Aubade for Museums

museum piece aubade
aubade you're not allowed to touch
priceless aubade
painted aubade
sculpture aubade
weird video in a dark little side room aubade

Allen Ginsberg Aubade VII

please come fast to this aubade
this aubade needs you the way
a fish needs water
sudden aubade
communist aubade
fascist aubade
aubade everyone can get behind
aubade with no allegiance
Arkansas aubade
nightmare aubade

Nightmare Aubades

nightmare aubade
aubade you wake up from in a cold sweat
aubades that are uncomfortably similar to nocturnes
monstrous aubades
tornado aubades
the garden we dream of aubade
sex dream aubade
using dream aubade

Ex-Girlfriend Aubades

aubade for making out on Art Hill
aubade for making out in the monkey house
aubade for moving the bed with our lovemaking
aubade for stupidly living together
sex in Tower Grove Park aubade
sex within view of a wine bar aubade
sex that is memorable & sex that isn't aubade
Borderline Personality Disorder aubade
visiting her in the hospital aubade
losing my mind with jealousy aubade

Not an Aubade

the rain falls
& the rain falls
& the
rain falls

Allen Ginsberg Aubade VIII

lovely aubades
forgotten aubades
aubades for her
aubades for nobody
smooth aubades
confounding aubades

Confusing Aubades

confusing aubades
aubades that don't quite add up
aubades in the red
aubades that are left turns into wildness

Wilderness Aubades

aubades that can survive for months at a time in the wilderness
aubades you don't wanna mess with
tough aubades
aubades with shotguns
hunter aubades
poacher aubades
aubades that kill elephants
aubades with whiskers
big & tall aubades

John Berryman Aubade

lying down looking at the aubade
it's a cruel aubade we live in
this aubade is a double agent for the nocturnes
unsightly growth aubade
mask aubade
torturous aubade
disrobing aubade
can there ever be enough aubades?
aubades you make a pilgrimage to
terrible aubades
aubades the editor let slide
vague aubades

Vague Aubades

let's go get some aubades
I am aubade
you should have aubade me
dumb aubades
challenged aubades
wet aubades
living aubades
aubades in tanks
aubades with umbrellas
vague aubades
aubades that don't mean anything
aubades with no objective correlative in sight

Rusting Aubades

rusting aubades
metal aubades
sharp aubades
aubades that are sword canes
aubades that work like armor
chain mail aubades

Aubade Written at the Port of Darryl

tugboat aubade
river's edge aubade
barge aubade
aubade rubble
broken heap of aubades at the river's edge
aubade shards at the river's edge
driftwood aubade at the river's edge
aubades lapping up at the river's edge
aubade bags & aubade cans & bits of
aubade that don't
look like much of anything
aubade tiles
seven-story nursing aubade at the river's edge
aubade anaphora at the river's edge
aubades of downtown St. Louis as viewed from the river's edge
auabady sky at the river's edge
ugly brown aubade
aubade I've baptized people in

Detente Aubade

I was once the leader of an aubade called Detente
I founded Detente to propagate the aubades
(these are the aubades)
& to defeat Darryl
but Darryl
defeated us
it ended the way all aubades end:
BETRAYAL

Four Strings Nocturne

nocturne written at Four Strings in Soulard
nocturne of the generous pour
jazz nocturne
nocturne pizza
roll of paper towels nocturne
granite counter nocturne
Jack Daniels neat nocturne
Budweiser coasters nocturne

Rollercoaster Nocturne

rollercoaster nocturne
up & down & then up again nocturne
it's every nocturne for himself out here
post-apocalypse nocturne

In Watermelon Sugar Nocturne

if jazz guitar is playing
that is my nocturne
if you're drinking alone
that is my nocturne
if it's cold & rainy outside but warm in here
that is my nocturne
if you're OK with how the nocturnes are going
that is my nocturne

Christianity Nocturne

robbing Peter to pay the nocturne
nocturne bibles
nocturne Deuteronomy
the catechism of the Catholic Nocturne
advent nocturne
prince of peace nocturne
Dead Sea Scrolls nocturne
Vatican bank nocturne
nocturne crucifixion
official nocturne of the Roman Empire
nocturne schism
martyr nocturnes
nocturne saints
hymnal nocturnes
nocturne monks
Opus Nocturne

Restaurant Nocturne

busser nocturne
bartender nocturne
dishwasher nocturne
head chef nocturne
manager nocturne
server nocturne
patron nocturne

Melodramatic Nocturne

theatrical nocturne
melodramatic nocturne
nocturne gesticulations
nocturnes jumping up & down
nocturne really making a scene
sobbing nocturne
hungry nocturne
nocturne taking their pants off
& waving them like a flag

In Nocturnes We Trust

in nocturnes we trust
e pluribus nocturne
nocturne currency
bank of nocturne
assassinated nocturne

Ted Berrigan Nocturne

ambiguous nocturnes
dark nocturnes
nocturne leaves
deciduous nocturnes
piercing nocturnes
nocturne lances
incidental nocturnes
jolly good fellow nocturnes
island nocturne
womanly nocturne
phosphorescent nocturnes
nocturne taking a bath
rubber nocturnes
baby nocturnes
cowboy nocturnes
summer nocturne
silk nocturne
green nocturne
nocturne mountains
nocturne sonnets

Nocturne Sonnet

goes a sinful nocturne needing no meadow
ebbing nocturne in heaven
removed nocturne snapped in half
the last time we met we met at a nocturne
nocturne elves, nothing is a nocturne, wayward nocturne
I met a traveler from a nocturne land
much have I traveled in nocturne realms
the nocturne of thanks & praise
heard nocturnes are sweet
nocturne shining in the sky like a zeppelin
the bloody nocturne at noon
nocturne criminals, nocturne mariners
one nocturne the more, nocturne library
nocturne misgivings, far off nocturne, burning nocturne

The Aubade We Need but Not the Aubade We Want

physical aubade
sophisticated aubade
technical aubade
aubade velocity
aubade laws
reliable aubade
contingent aubade
aubade experience
suffering aubade
aubade climate
meditative aubade
aubade at the void
project aubade
Pruitt-Igoe aubade
aubade modernism
controlled aubades
imploded aubades
deceitful aubades
aubade politicians
plural aubades
aubade maps
aubade residents
aubades that raise questions
combined aubades
aubade caterpillars
butterfly aubades

Tucker's Nocturne

Tucker's nocturne
Knob Creek nocturne
shoutout nocturne
callout culture nocturne
meeting up with friends nocturne
nocturne for new friends
nocturne for fast friends
nocturne without music
muted televisions nocturne
ample selection of whiskey nocturne
big-breasted nocturne
hurry up nocturne
nocturne popcorn
overheard snippets of nocturne
South Broadway nocturne
"sometimes I wish I was a nocturne
so I could fly around & shit on people's heads"
taking off see ya nocturne
geriatric nocturne
nocturne jukebox
having not seen someone in a very long time nocturne
ring ring better answer the nocturne
I'm used to people screaming "nocturne!"
look who just walked in the nocturne
you got a lot of nocturne showing your face in here
you better come & talk to me nocturne
throwing a nocturne
nocturne fit
tantrum nocturne
toddler nocturne
nocturne yeah
money talks nocturne
nocturne lubrication
offensive nocturne
nocturne goals
nocturne defense
nocturne pollsters
bumming nocturnes from the bartender
handout nocturnes
Social Security Nocturne
flag at half-staff nocturne
nocturne revolutionaries

police nocturne
nocturne saints
nocturne friends
friends that are nocturnes
you don't have to nocturne
what are you, a nocturne?
nocturne citizens
The Republic of Nocturne
Rick & Morty nocturne
have you met my buddy Nocturne?
Nocturne, meet Korina

Midterm Election Nocturne

the nocturnes are in
Democrats take the House but lose the Nocturne
I don't know what to say
it's disappointing
but I guess that's
the name of the nocturne
everybody loses

Jorie Graham Nocturne

take my hand
let us write this nocturne together
my sister bought me Jorie Graham's Nocturne last Christmas
this comes from that
the future of nocturnes
someone should pay me for these nocturnes
deforestation nocturne
complete nocturne
tightened up nocturne
nocturnes drying on clotheslines
swarm of nocturnes
let's talk about these nocturnes
how do you think they're going so far?
I'm getting overly attached to my nocturnes
this is only the third day of nocturnes
soon I will be free of the yoke of the nocturnes
you must help me out with these nocturnes
I can't do it without you
whimpering nocturnes
delirious nocturnes
an interview with a nocturne
well-organized nocturnes
phantom nocturnes
changed forever by nocturnes
self-conscious nocturnes
nocturnes going through puberty
hesitating nocturnes
meaty nocturnes
nocturnes that look out the window
chained up nocturnes
whimsical nocturnes
one nocturne after another
nocturnes floating downstream
I don't even know how many nocturnes there are
no one does
consequential nocturnes
nocturne afterlife
hopeful nocturnes
nocturnes programmed to carry out various household tasks
I am alone with my nocturnes
it feels like there have always been nocturnes
immediate nocturne

nocturnes that can talk
real nocturnes
the destruction of nocturnes
nocturne gatherings
crosshatched nocturnes
dysfunctional nocturnes
dystopian nocturne
nocturne characters

Compromised Nocturnes

compromised nocturnes
foundations of nocturne
fossilized nocturnes
nocturnes that have been around the block
nocturne lemonade
little girls & boys asking for nocturnes for Christmas
cast aside nocturnes
nocturnes that have bearing on the discourse

Frank O'Hara Nocturne

nocturnes only just now realizing their potential
cold nocturnes
proud nocturnes
nocturnes that have errands to run
nocturnes that go BOOM
approaching nocturnes
nocturnes that don't get along with aubades
simple nocturnes
mint-flavored nocturnes
nocturnes that lead you on
nocturne parades
nocturnes that know how to ski
snowballing nocturnes
prepositional phrase nocturnes
nocturne verbs
spectacular nocturnes
nocturnes that wait for you to get home
faint trace of a nocturne

Nocturne on Aubades

nocturnes are very different from aubades
nocturnes & aubades are so different they can't procreate
nocturnes & aubades generally avoid each other
usually nocturnes don't even talk about aubades
nocturnes wish there wasn't a need for aubades
nocturnes would get rid of the aubades if they could
nocturnes hate aubades

The Fingers of Nocturne

the fingers of
of nocturne keep
at it until
they are exhausted

the fingers of nocturne the
agents of nocturne firmly
believe they are doing
god's work

the fingers
of nocturne know
that aubades are coming
soon

the
fingers of nocturne do
their best their very
best to do

what must be said

Adrienne Rich Nocturne

lesser of two evils nocturne
crowded nocturne
it's a nocturne, not a choice
nocturne abortions
continental nocturne
Black Panther nocturne
stained glass nocturne
airy nocturne
sensual nocturne
foraging for nocturnes
nocturnes that live in the basement
rectangular nocturnes
common nocturne
nocturne in denial

Howard Shore's Nocturne

soaring nocturne
nocturne choir
symphonic nocturne
nocturne of light & darkness
nocturne as good as the book
nocturne worthy of Tolkien
elvish nocturne
nocturne separated into movements
awe-inspiring nocturne
battle nocturnes
the nocturne that started it all
the nocturne that will finish it
prophetic nocturne
almost biblical nocturne
nocturne that reminds you of Yosemite
nocturne of Rohan
nocturne wizard
nocturne halls
magical nocturnes
one nocturne to rule them all

Marching Aubades

marching aubades
aubades in lockstep
aubades that know how to take orders
how can I help you aubade
fast food aubades
minimum wage aubades
union aubades
aubade corporations

Aubade on the Verge of Being a Nocturne

aubade wine
fine aubades
velvet aubades
aubade noir
aubade read aloud
aubade megaphone
aubade protesters
aubade riot police
aubade snipers
aubade gas
aubade handcuffs
Homeland Security aubades
aubade memories

Aubade Written at MoKaBe's

hip-hop aubade
aubade libretto
later aubades
suspect aubade
aubades that resemble gas stations
novice aubade
aubade commotion
aubade sex scene
undiscovered aubade
aubade castle
confessional aubade
aubades in vain
aubade warning
war hawk aubade
soothing aubade
aubade coupons
aubade duet
broken aubades
clocktower aubade
aubades in hiding
aubade motifs
freakish aubade
aubade sandwich
aubade witches
cellular aubade
aubade basketball
aubade open house
aubade smoothie
miniature aubades
aubades in the minority
aubade recital
occasional aubades
aubade ballad
aubade queen
merciful aubade
aubade quartet
aubades that urge you to do things
buxom aubade
aubade prince
aubade conference
meritorious aubade
aubade marquee

conventional aubade
just a few more aubades
operatic aubade
aubade prioress
official aubade
aubade magistrate
aubade caliphate
Islamic aubade

Lemont's Aubade

appreciative aubade
born & raised in aubade
Gateway Arch aubade
aubade high school
dog aubade
ecstasy aubade
black aubade
homeless aubade
$500 worth of aubade
incarcerated aubade
Bon Terre prison aubade
workhouse aubade
the best aubade
it was the best of aubades, it was the worst of aubades
radical aubade
fascinating aubade
first kiss aubade
ashtray aubade
most people are loving aubade

Nocturne from the Great Operas

a return to nocturnes
nocturne garden
symbol nocturnes
nocturne lamps
contemplative nocturne
suicidal nocturne
fourth watch of the night nocturne
walk on water nocturne
miraculous nocturne
before there were nocturnes there were aubades
or is it the other way around?
nominal nocturnes
cf. the Nocturnes
nocturne careers
nocturne initiation
hockey nocturne
Irish nocturne
nocturne numbers
mosaic nocturne
nocturne graffiti
unresolved nocturne
nocturne that would do anything for an aubade
nocturne whose lover is an aubade
Juliet nocturne
mock nocturne
nocturne masks
flaky nocturnes
dermatology nocturne
successful nocturne
two-car garage nocturne
nocturne cemetery
nocturne epitaph
pneumonic nocturne
pneumatic nocturne
nocturne numerology
nocturne stars
satellite nocturnes
nocturnes we can barely see even with the most powerful telescopes
paparazzi nocturne
celebrity sex tape nocturne
reality nocturne
nocturne advertisements

nocturnes to believe in
nocturne achievements
nocturne sirens
holiday nocturnes
nocturne t-shirts
cruise nocturnes
nocturne missiles
nocturne missives
nocturne you miss when it's gone
nocturne K-hole
illegal nocturnes
TSA nocturne
nocturne terrorist
I'm right & they're nocturne
nocturne pedophiles
FBI nocturnes
disturbing nocturnes
disturbed nocturnes
nocturne straitjacket
schizophrenic nocturne
21st Century Nocturne Man
the court of the crimson nocturne

Fourth Wall Nocturne

nocturne that breaks the fourth wall
epistemological nocturne
nocturne alchemy
Midas nocturne
David Lynch's nocturne
Angelo Badalamenti's nocturne
nobody's nocturne
nocturne way out of proportion
nocturne Bob
scary nocturne
nocturne separated into episodes

Nocturne Separated into Episodes

Nocturne 1, Episode 1
in this groundbreaking pilot nocturne,
two nocturnes compete for the attention of
homecoming queen & everybody is
shocked when both nocturnes are
found dead

Nocturne 1, Episode 2
a nocturne has developed between
the homecoming queen & her
high school English teacher; her mom
considers getting a nocturne

Nocturne 1, Episode 3
strange nocturnes begin showing up;
the nocturne of the football team
posits a theory about the murder of his
two closest nocturnes

Nocturne 1, Episode 4
the homecoming queen's dad files a nocturne
against the city council; the chief of
nocturnes discovers a clue

unfortunately the nocturne
got cancelled so we'll
never know who done the nocturne

Narcotics Anonymous Nocturne

serenity nocturne
nocturne hugs
sharing my nocturne
nocturne recovery
wanting to die nocturne
playing the tape through to the end nocturne
sponsor nocturne
nocturne addicts
clean nocturne
nocturne relapse
productive member of society nocturne

A to Z Nocturne

able-bodied nocturne
betrothal nocturne
catering nocturne
dessert nocturne
elevator nocturne
frustrated nocturne
gravity's nocturne
nocturne home
idealistic nocturne
juvenile nocturne
nocturne kids
nocturne lobotomy
materialist nocturne
nib nocturne
oscillating nocturne
pastry nocturne
nocturne, question mark?
nocturne railroad
sick nocturne
nocturne teddy bear
umbrella nocturne
vascular nocturne
weird nocturne
nocturne x-ray
yard full of nocturnes
zilch nocturne

State of the Nocturne Address

my fellow nocturnes!
three days ago I began writing nocturnes
I come before you today to say
that the state of the nocturne is strong!
but lest our nocturnes ever become
dull & repetitive
we must constantly re-evaluate them
so it is with great pride that I can announce
that we're going to stop writing nocturnes
for the day
& come back at it fresh tomorrow

Oh All Right, One More Nocturne

I am not a nocturne, nor was meant to be
suppose I make you a nocturne you can't refuse?
a brooding nocturne
a Wallace Stevens nocturne
a nocturne you can almost see & hear & touch & roll up & smoke it
nocturne weather
whispered nocturnes
animal nocturnes
nocturnes we've seen before
revisited nocturnes
oppressive nocturne
abstract nocturne
a nocturne you have to carry down to the beach
because it can't walk anymore
the lifespan of a nocturne
the exoskeleton of a nocturne & a nocturne's beating heart
musty nocturne
nocturne with mothballs in the pockets
stolen nocturne
nocturne bicycle
nocturne horizon
nocturnes that don't exist yet

doubt creeps into the nocturnes
is it good? is it right?
goodnight?

Aubade Written in Professor Kimbrell's Class

Freddie Mercury aubade
nails on a chalkboard aubade
classroom aubade
well-caffeinated aubade
aubades in the meantime
unfurled aubade
dilated aubade
birthing coach aubade
aubade that starts shit
shutting down the aubade
I should pay attention

Mass Transit Aubade

The aubades are in deep trouble. Despite their good intentions, some of the aubades' best friends appear bent on making matters worse. These nocturne advocates are obsessed by the assumption that the aubade's cost, comfort, & convenience will not be matched by the nocturne. This unnecessarily pessimistic assumption has led many of our aubade planners down blind alleys from which we are only now beginning to escape. Today, aubades carry a diminished fraction of the market—less than forty-eight percent of the poem—& their share continues to decline. One group of aubade pessimists has simply given up all hope of substantially improving the aubade picture. Instead, they have tried to turn our attention, & all our resources, to the worthy but limited task of furnishing service to those without nocturnes, & to those dwindling numbers still reading the poem. This group would be thrilled with a market share approaching fifty percent. A second group of aubade pessimists has adopted a strategy designed to limit use of the nocturne. This group looks to government to force imposition of the same traditional aubade systems that have failed again & again to attract significant readership on their own merits. These pessimists are asking the federal government to pay the cost of their multi-billion dollar traditional aubades, to pick up the huge operating subsidy tab, & to impose tough limitations on the use of the nocturne. The only problem is it won't work. The public is not likely to accept being forced back into a substantially inferior mode of poetry, but it might accept some limits on nocturnes if attractive alternatives are available. Hopefully this aubade will encourage the pessimists among us to raise their expectations concerning the future role of aubades in our poem. No miracles are promised, but it offers hope of a real poetical choice, rather than obsolete aubades or more nocturnes.

Prisoner Victor Nelson's Aubade

The men in the aubades are like the common men everywhere. Now & then one meets a quick & intelligent mind in the aubades, some man who has fallen into the net of the aubade by some one mischance or through the slipshod weakness of his make-up. Such men have written of aubade life, but their words are too deeply personal to be of real value...

Aubade Roads

Aubades are of such increasing interest & importance that I gladly accepted the invitation to write an account of their prehistoric & historic development, the principles of their construction & maintenance, & their value in national policy. Great Britain during the past ten years has spent on aubades five hundred million pounds, in addition to the local expenditures. The credit for making the first system of aubades has been long & authoritatively given to the Carthaginians. The future of aubade policy raises a problem of special concern for the British Empire. Is it better to continue the building of nocturnes, or to regard nocturnes as obsolete & put our trust in aubades?

Labor Aubade

The worker, the thinker, the student, the statesman, & the capitalist are all forced, by the pressure of events, to consider the Aubade Movement & the Aubade Problem. The history of the Aubade Movement is the history of civilization. If we would comprehend our present aubade problems, we must carefully study the conditions out of which they have grown. The modern aubade is a historical product. There is a special difficulty in the way of getting all the facts in regard to the history of the aubade in past times, owing to the circumstance that history has nearly always been written by the nocturnes.

Men & Machines & Aubades

Certain aubades hold that
nocturnes are
enslaving us.

The first thing I hear in
the morning
is a
nocturne.

Elizabeth Bishop's Nocturne

this is going to be a giant nocturne
a nocturne that'll win medals
a nocturne that'll never crumble & tumble
a nocturne with touching details
a refreshing nocturne
a nocturne that if you set it on fire it wouldn't burn
nevertheless, a nocturne
not one of those weak nocturnes
not a nocturne that needs to be patched up later
a nocturne that reads YOU
a nocturne that inspires you to do the dishes
the nocturne of the century
not some solemn nocturne!
a Babylon nocturne
a neat row of sugar maple nocturnes
a nocturne that'll leave you sore
when it's time to write aubades again
a nocturne that doesn't pity itself
not an infant nocturne; an elder nocturne
a nocturne that endures in the face of adversity & haters
a nocturne as knowledgeable as an almanac is
& as your father seemed, once
a nocturne that keeps time better than a Swiss watch
a nocturne more like an aunt than an uncle
a nocturne that's good for you, like vegetables
a city nocturne
a nocturne as delicate as plates used only occasionally
but as strong as the ones you use every day
a nocturne that will make you orgasm
not the ghost of a nocturne—an immortal nocturne!
a nocturne not in the least bit similar to slush
a nocturne more like Antarctica
a nocturne that outshines the sun
& outloves your mother
not a nocturne disloyal like the Rams
a nocturne like the Cardinals
not a nocturne that robs you;
rather, a nocturne that donates you a kidney
A dream nocturne. Not a nightmare nocturne.
This is a nocturne that can speak
in complete sentences
(when it wants to).

This is not a nocturne that shows you her breasts at a party; this is a nocturne that you take out to a nice dinner.

Gerard Manley Hopkins Nocturne

Now this nocturne is different.
It's a tomb nocturne, a swearing nocturne, an evermore nocturne.
Victorious, this nocturne
keeps the faith.
This is no heretic nocturne, let me tell you.
'Tis a free nocturne, a stern pious churchy nocturne.
A monk nocturne. A drear nocturne.
This nocturne is discordant but blessed,
painful but destined for greatness.
This nocturne got soul.
This nocturne got fear.
This nocturne got words like
"fraught"
&
"ere"
&
"purify."
To hear this nocturne, to pause on it til
the molten hour, is to
vex oneself. With piteous dismay
a quivering pennon (what is
a pennon?*), an intense
crystalline misty blossoming,
deflowers me. Unbound
daylight & waxen
colors, stupidly
praised, afflict us. (For we are
in this together.) In hell,
the crowns & "why!"s & coldness
(or heat, depending which mythology you subscribe to, if
any) meet in the lonely
acres. Waterfall noons & effrontery
sweet sweetness, pearl
stars treasure flocks trees,
Etc.

*Pennon: another word for "pennant."

Nocturne from Good Old Robert Frost

someone else's nocturne
a nocturne everybody will laugh at
a nocturne that knows my name
a nocturne that knows its own name at least, like a dog
a nocturne who's afraid of other nocturnes
a nocturne half as big as the previous nocturne
a nocturne you can put on your dashboard like a little plastic angel
a nocturne that's always looking over its shoulder
a nocturne that doesn't
live very long
a nocturne that couldn't spell "earthquake"
if the Pulitzer Prize depended on it
a nocturne that isn't similar to a diamond
a nocturne that has no business mentioning diamonds
a nocturne with no progeny or prospects
a finite nocturne
underdog nocturne
the village nocturne
a--halting nocturne
a nocturne that just doesn't get it
a nocturne that I wouldn't choose
if someone asked me to
carve it in fresh cement
a nocturne that takes so many smoke breaks it gets fired

Liar Nocturne

liar nocturne
Pinocchio nocturne
nocturne workers
nocturne that needs a crew to run it
nocturne iceberg
Mexico nocturne
disastrous camping trip with my ex-nocturne
cuddling nocturne
sweet nothings nocturne
unbuttoned nocturne
nocturnes hanging out for all to see
hairless nocturnes
pink nocturnes
nocturnes you can touch & nocturnes you can't

Aubade Written at Tower Grove Park

pavilion aubades
memory aubades
sex behind a tree aubade
dogs being walked aubade
short aubade

Paradise Lost Aubade

man's first (original) aubade
that forbidden aubade
aubade that brought death into the world
til one greater aubade restored us
good shepherd aubade
aubade hell
creator of aubades
aubades in revolt
aubade angels
aubade war
vanquished aubades
aubade crimes
glorious aubade
aubade ruin
dubious aubade
unconquerable aubade
advancing aubade
eternal aubade
aubade providence
aubade flames
aubade Satan (Darryl)

Darryl's Aubade

it's the only thing I really know:
Darryl cannot be trusted
Darryl hates the aubades
Darryl doesn't stand a chance against the aubades
Darryl has allied himself with the nocturnes
Darryl is the nocturnes' secret weapon
the aubades keep Darryl awake at night
the aubades will win in the end
the aubades hit Darryl in his weak spot
the aubades are scientifically formulated
to kill Darryl but not us
Darryl doesn't stand a chance against the aubades

Aubade from the Sonnets of John Berryman

lightning aubade
aubade voyages
aubades on the level
aubades that last just fifteen minutes
knock on the door aubade
feverish aubade
aubade at dawn
watching the aubades go by

Aubade Not from Pastiche

mechanical aubades
pop-up aubades
aubades you have to clean up after
aubades you read in the waiting room
aubade for my sister
aubade cadavers
aubades in pawnshops
aubade assembly line
aubades made in China
knockoff aubades
aubade hustlers
aubade pimps
bars that don't have a jukebox
because they only play aubades
doctors that use an aubade instead of a stethoscope
dentists that use aubades to clean your teeth
lawyers submitting aubades in lieu of closing arguments
wars fought with aubades as ammunition
aubade-industrial complex
aubade legislators
deregulatory aubades
aubade filibusters
motion to write another aubade?

Stream of Consciousness Aubade

aubade vehicles
aubades in space
green screen aubades
aubade conspiracy theories
9/11 aubade
false flag aubade
Alex Jones aubade
gun control aubade
aubade assassins
the aubade is truly mightier than the sword
oral aubades
naval aubades
jetty aubades
lighthouse aubades
aubade sunscreen
aubade carcinogens
nuclear aubade
aubade submarines
aubade in disputed territory

Cucumber Nocturne

cucumber nocturne
adult nocturne
strobe lights nocturne
nocturne seizure
bedwetting nocturne
nocturne Boy Scouts
nocturne knives
nocturne bondage
fetish nocturne
nocturne nipples
baby nocturne
undressed nocturne
nocturne zippers
rural nocturne

Theodore Roethke's Nocturne

giving out nocturnes to people who will want them
nocturnes for true love
nocturnes for me
transcending nocturnes
lush nocturnes
the nocturnes that always end up on the bottom
nocturne in soft light
nocturne coming closer

Evaluating the Nocturnes

at what point are there enough nocturnes?
are the nocturnes working?
I must score the nocturnes
troubleshoot the nocturnes
exterminate the inferior nocturnes
clean up the nocturnes
tinker with the nocturnes
until such a time as
I have something new to work on

Andrew Marvell's Nocturne

nocturne pestilence
magnetic nocturne
stately nocturne
nocturne midwife
unfrequented nocturne
nocturne spoils
nocturne armpits
halcyon nocturnes

The Last Aubade

this is the last aubade
no more
enough
the end
the conclusion
the resolution
the cigarette after the orgasm

GABRIEL BRIAN BOONE, REPUBLICAN

I will have more to say about this highly political
balustrade in later chapters; it is likely that we shall
know in a moment whether Europe & the United States
stand looking out the window. Make no mistake. Given
the power of central banks to hemorrhage money,
we find that a profound change has occurred in Gabriel.

It is interesting to observe him whisper loudly in the saloon.
It is also interesting to observe the ratio between Gabriel's
cottage fifty years ago & the two-thirds bankruptcy of 1797.
The next day we all said, "There is no doubt that the
minimum wage plays an essential role in the formation
& evolution of his nervousness." It is our sacred duty

to have ourselves buried in a pile of money. The world
has clearly changed a great deal since last week. The liquidity
created by Gabriel's lemonade spill has its advantages.
One evening a substantial number of people went into
the drawing room. This is what Britain did to
speed away the time. Are we really certain that

the room was lighted by a half-dozen candles? To sum up,
I persisted in the two forces of divergence. There exists a hierarchy
of wealth, & it is not our business to criticize it.
Available historical data suggests that Gabriel
cleared his throat. To an even greater extent than myself
Gabriel felt like a plucked rooster after doing his taxes.

Freed from regulation, Gabriel stank of beer &
very rapid economic growth. There are vacant lots on
either side of his shitty house. This is explained by
three factors: Russians, women, & a vague sense of
melancholy. Until three weeks ago, Gabriel was
characterized by short-term volatility. Praise

the free market from whom all blessings come!
The vast majority of people have seen at least one
hit musical. Organizations that depend primarily on
Gabriel invariably get soft. There is nothing natural or
spontaneous about the guy. Insofar as Gabriel
wishes he had never entered the funhouse,

the future is complex & uncertain. My lack of excitement
counterbalanced our common fate. Apportioning
blame to the toolshed has its limits. The world
plays an important part in Gabriel; at nine o'clock
there is no doubt that Gabriel will find himself in a
terrible predicament. In other words: FUCK.

EVERYTHING

1

O ends of times! O Master of the breathing earth! Again the sentiment: I remember the death of a tree. Beautiful snowglobes of bucolic futures, sold for a wet kiss. All those smiling refusals; in tatters, I'm going this way. Unsung journeys, over-sung temples: let me tell the story of ripened beach summers. One might
stop talking
all love
tombward sped
but until
the kings & queens
are blown away like
gray clouds, the dream will carry on its idiocy, & the rain will keep the cathedral steps dangerous to walk on, & I will feel crazy, & all but dead.

2

My fire I saw spread. Still there is the shape, occasional & obligatory, of my own skull. Learn to wait. Beyond the bad magic, the last hour of drunkenness casually stands up to leave. Yes; the stars struggle too with daybreak. The fountain & the children's voices idly, like old friends, tip their hats to each other. The heart
nudges the
totality of
body
toward humanity.
Great is the
empire of
loneliness & sacred is the unbroken road. Everything, in the morning, needs a shave. Only a few fragments of glances shall I be able to render.

3

If the horsemen interrupt the students, all at once the clouds will take a rejoicing shape. This form has no homework, no funerals to attend, no halfway-house to suffer in, as Everything suffers. Throughout the litany of the names of drowning victims I wonder what I would furnish a meadow with if I had a meadow.

The aristocrat
holds up
the shield of
his lyrical
bank account
against

the dispassionate mumbles of the executioner. The sea, which we dread, whispers at the still point, & does not know the whirl of leaves.

4

A dream: curled up by a bay window, I am watching the rain drench a gymnast who seems to have been caught off guard by the well-forecast storm. Sadness: bubbling up like acid reflux, unable to eat, searching horoscopes for hope &, for generations, declaiming questionable wisdom. Desire, my friends,
even for
Everything,
revolves
around
admitting that
the higher
the height, the faller the fall. It is twilight. It is a proper wife. It is an experience everyone has. It is endless. It is Everything. It is mine.

5

I bind my sins for kindling. When I am in the mountains, I look at wildflowers but I do not care enough to find out the make & model, as Everything would. In the afternoons, I hope for the best. Try pretending your character has not been baselessly indicted by communists. Avoid the street known for its causal weeping. In a tragic scene,

a pair of
eyebrows
are raised
at an old
woman's
immense narrative.

In all four corners of the room, the story echoes like the plight of the homeless in a locked-up church. And in the desert, there is a group of people playing cards. (One of them is Everything.)

6

Suddenly (but not without warning) a pattern forms. Treasonous worlds, stripped of their worldliness, beg for scraps at my doorstep. Soon my house is clogged with former worlds. They have such stories, too many to relay. "You're right," I said to one of the worlds, whose name is Everything. "This world is not really that small at all."

They are not
insects
but they are certainly
very small.
Most of them
stay up all night,

better than dogs for company but not as easy to feed. They don't know what they want. To them, the most precious thing is their memory. And they don't remember Everything.

7

I was hiding from a strawman when a rabbit appeared in the cedar closet. It started laughing & I saw its molars. There was nowhere to run. "What do you want? Why are you laughing?" The rabbit stopped laughing, said, "Everything is not possible," & then continued laughing. "The freedom
to rejoice
is predicated on
the freedom to not rejoice.
Therefore,
—uh-oh!"
It was the strawman.
The rabbit addressed the strawman: "Make me a chocolate cake, for it is my birthday."
The strawman refused.

8
Maybe I am deluded in thinking that our bodies, clothed as they are in luxury, would be indigestible. I decided against learning the art of gardening from Everything, but it was nice of him to offer. I have stopped carrying my fucks on my person; I just leave them in the car with my handgun & my expired insurance card. The pitcher
gets
distracted
by a
naked man
who runs out in the field
yelling,
"They told me if I was patient, I would become an astronaut. Do I look like an astronaut?!" I often tell this story to a pair of boots.

9

Regretting sex, she leans up on her elbow. "More manpower would be required," she says to Everything, regretting that too. Everything fingers her for a few minutes. That doesn't work either. It's a bad sign. Birds are chirping out in the October morning. She goes out for breakfast with him, which she does not regret. Time after time
this happens.
They danced,
once; now
they are Nothing
to each other.
Ferociously
Nothing. Everything remembers her giving him a blowjob by the river once. That was nice. The homeless people thought so, too.

10

Like a glad look on the face of Everything opening a door for you, the rain came down, washing off the sidewalk chalk & my cigarette ashes. We try not to break down. We play with our dogs. We avoid producing new wisdom. We think little of the dead. We ripen & make the branch sag. Soon we
will fall
on Newton's head
& gravity will
be invented.
And we will
be eaten.
Or we will lie in the weeds & talk of happiness. It follows that our mortality is YUM. And then I think of staying here with Everything.

11

Consider Everything. Lean on him when you have no one else to lean on. Compliment the lady who has just buried her dog. Let Everything guess what happened to you when you made a reservation at a nice restaurant with a false name. Everything we write, Everything we take naked delight in, Everything we

imagine

is like a

wall

which we

build to

separate ourselves from

Death. I swear by him. And Everything never runs out, never runs off, never runs into me (because Everything is already with me). And Everything is not meaningless.

12

Naked in an armchair by the fire on a cold night, Everything looks for something on which to wipe his eyeglasses. Reborn, you hide no longer from Death. Or rather, you hide playfully, letting him find you, & giggling when he does. I still remember the time I almost drowned: what a sailboat! Speak of

Eternity &

you will

experience

the same thing

you will experience if

you speak of Death:

Everything there is to feel, felt from a distance, like watching a house a few blocks away burn to the ground. If you go too close, you get too hot, & if you get too hot, well, you're hot, & it's uncomfortable.

13

Do you smell Everything I dumped in the wheelbarrow to take care of later? A teacher, wanting to avoid jury duty, tells the prosecutor he was sent from the future to educate the bloodshot eyes of people who never learned to dance. "For the sake of the children, we have to dream." They dismissed him. Hurling

Everything
into a lovely
leafy green
darkness
I shout,
 "Remember the Alamo!"

Isolated choirs sing of the serpent far from the ears of sinners, & old-fashioned women admire not the galaxy but children's costumes, & you must do one or the other.

14

Death trots along to halt the voyage of a man who is averse to smoke. Piece by piece a ballerina assembles a puzzle. In the puzzle, there is a farmhouse, & children crying outside of it. She is my darling. Toying with a paintbrush & a do-it-yourself birdhouse, Everything blows a kiss to a woman who is knowledgeable about methods of torture.
You forget
your manners
at a
museum
which specializes in
statues of snakes.
Better go back for them. Everything asks me if I want to go for a swim. I say maybe but Everything insists. The water is cold. As I am adjusting, treading water, a heron lands nearby. We decide to name the heron after a beekeeper we know. It's the least we can do.

15

My sister says she is bored so I offer her a cigar. I explain that a potbellied man from the Cretaceous period puked on my shoes. A spider crawls onto her & she becomes so upset she forgets about the cigar. She doesn't seem to want it. We're both wearing red but it's just a coincidence. I go outside to smoke the cigar & Everything is fog.
Pain is
a product of
life. So is
Everything,
it seems.
I wonder if
the spider I killed had any thoughts on the topic. I remark to Everything that we may have killed a renowned spider philosopher. We debate what sort of philosophy spiders would favor. Who can say?

16

Softly down the stairs I go, reciting this mantra: "We are morally right, we are morally right, we are morally right." I leave the parking garage at street level & catch passerby phrases like lightning bugs on a summer night. Everything exhales loudly. It is midnight. The night crowd. I recall
how
life
became
a punishment.
Wisdom isn't
Everything.
I long for sensuous knowledge of another, any other really. At my side Everything dangles a dollar over a trumpet case, waiting to be moved.

17

Everything was not proud of literally biting my darling's nipple off. I used to feel like my life was a film. Now I feel like my life is an outrageous piece of furniture that Everything wants to sit on. The landscape, an illusion, breaks: my schooling prepared me for division, but not this. Injected progress

makes Everything

turn

red.

While I

shine a light on

a sunshaft,

my darling dreams that I have died, & that the most voracious men have struck up a tune called "The Kingdom of the Mouse" outside the tavern.

HOPE: A LAMENT

You too hate your faults, moving to
find a substitute for Jim; the cathedral
is several blocks away. If only Patrick knew
his destiny! Women like men to be
torn, sad, & weather-beaten. Mother tells me
that outer space is coquettishly reproachful.

We must die because on our long walk home
the song we struck up was dragged out
groggy-eyed for copyright violation. A lament
didn't just happen to accept control of our throats:
nowadays, regal ballads have been replaced by
offensive weeping. We're getting nourishment

from bluffing, youth from listening to loud
music until there is a buzzing in our ears, conscience
from crossing the abyss, and we're getting along
wonderfully with everybody. And if, half
an hour later, a bell rings, we will realize how many
kids our age have already have their flesh cast in bronze.

Of course, this may be just music, an apocalyptic
passion between George & the nearest wench. Old
playmate of mine Kenny vaulted the railing & dropped
down onto the beach where someone had written "HOPE"
in the sand. I'm not pretending I haven't performed, day
after day, the most elaborate ceremonies of lamentation,

but I have a vision of looking myself in the mirror
& seeing my innermost self, & not hating it. Let's
forget I told you that. Seductive Oliver gave Charlie
a pomegranate; Charlie gave Oliver his bed. As they
bent & inflicted, the sun shone, & the sound of their
lovemaking echoed comically down the hall. You

have wasted your time totally. Symbolically,
the future remains submerged, asleep, but you
can still be amused by Penelope's laughter. The bloody
past & monastic gravity drown my lungs because,
out in the open, ghosts incommunicado pry into
my affairs. After Jim denied you, Patrick

patted you on the back & said, "Listen carefully.
God is definitely real. Perhaps I am being
old-fashioned, but poached eggs on toast are
very nice." And often Penelope gazed at Kenny in
wonder, wondering at his wonderful
lack of fear. We are all chasing

delight, wishing to be won over, on short notice
striding through the ruins. Unimaginably gradual
godlike dawns; flowers & flirtation, sometimes
unsubstantial but never disfiguring, sometimes
conscious but never enough to make you cry. You
may stand on solid ground with Patrick, but I

feel, in my solitude, filthy beyond words, terrified
of tomorrow, yet transforming my wicked ways
into stones which I then throw into the darkness.
Let me, Lord, be straight, & good, & not interested in
the myriad debaucheries. Death—is there any hope of
feeling nothing when it comes time? A dozen

painful memories: you've got to make up your
mind to leave them behind like so many possible
futures dashed on the flagstones. The extra
effort required to maintain a sort of freedom
utilizes a certain machinery to illuminate
our youth; to make matters worse, George

with outstretched arms has met a new
girl to inquisitively hop onto. The air
is full of smoke; Penelope held her glass
as if there were judgmental eyes on the walls
of Kenny's apartment. Now you feel how
I feel, now you don't, I can't keep up. Disappearing

hours--destruction, doesn't that matter to you?--stretch
out & withdraw at the speed of an express train. In
my element, my spirits rise & re-orient themselves like leaves
toward the sun. I go out for a walk & notice Jim
gently ebbing from our lives, saying things like,
"Come off it!" & "It had to happen." Primeval

rose-bush gazing into beloved eyes: harassed
& trembling, shy of each other, George & the next
girl bite & scratch each other to sleep, & a storm
comes & goes without any of them being the wiser.
What are we doing here? Journeying to heaven? Or
are we still rubbing our eyes in the mornings of our lives?

Even Kenny doesn't take my words to heart. Objecting
to the business with the statue, really vandalism
in general, I shook my head & walked home. For
a million years, losing armies have abruptly staggered
off the front page of history. Not unnaturally,
we push & shove our way onward, for reasons

strange to us. The sky had a quality like dancing
with the sun disappearing behind a pink cloud,
which itself was moving along a different path.
Yes; we are betrayed by our faces. It's not bewilderment;
it's a mask, beneath which lies Jim's inconsolable
grief. It wasn't easy, but it wasn't right the way

it was, he says. Enough of this for now.
What's the use? There is no question:
Patrick loves you. The others are happy. I have
yet to be. Fated fame for some, nasty shocks
for others, & this game I play with you
is one that either of us can choose to end.

IN FLOWERBED REPOSE

in flowerbed repose
I make eye contact with the blue sky
a car does not go past
a dog does not bark, my phone does not ring
no one notices me here, no one passes me on the sidewalk
a siren does not disturb me, it does not begin to rain
a war does not begin, a lemonade stand is not set up
no one knocks on the front door, the mail has already come
I just make eye contact with the sky
in flowerbed repose

PHALANX OF QUATRAINS AGAINST DARRYL

I HEREBY INVOKE HART CRANE AND JOHN BERRYMAN.

"And why do I often meet your visage here . . ."

"if we call/ Sometimes to one another . . ."

fortune-fled music wakes us in leaving
now unbetrayable, hot in a high place
glittering voices mouth sibilant dreams
wraiths laced-up, murmurs frame silence

one hand reaching out, marred by devotion
knowing what I know, debts of soul
having stumbled expensively into prophecy
the canyon joy-carved of our common craft

as if I am not like you, I go on: storm-versed,
but with watermelon days yet to come, & more love
charred from getting too close to Darryl
crownless but anointed, lusting after a gaze

my friends! all might be well; over the hill a
Muse, real, be yet pain! undelivered—deliver!
how regular, how regular—
"irregular & passionate"

WORDS

1
open & apparent meanings, our own, not for some
purpose fakely sailing; rather, with a word ("word") outfaces
reclining on our elbows, the enemy of all your graces
it must be that an old tear is not washed off yet

of dirt . . . it is not possible, the death or fall of kings
without evasion by a single faithful verity that sings
of watered flowers, all sorts of flowers; give me excess
of It, that my musing may immaculate soar above the view of men

the transformer, himself transformed, all the
titles of good fellowship having come to him,
chandelier his desert place, illustrious intimation of overheard conference
by perceiving the idea, make a crow a swan & a swan a crow, with confidence

2
they can only carry their base bribes in the freakish
ransomed straight & narrow nurse melancholy
mercy-lens no better than fools' balcony turning up of the right hand
a gift!—thus hath the candle, dulled to a halt, show in successful demand

words, words that will set you going like a fair lady's
entreaty to, amid marble & ultimately issuing, confect
many days together; so, let how still the evening is, can be, infect
out of the ash the lantern? out of the ash the ember, the spark, the not

fizzling out or dying; this is the game
prove you that any man, no exit, can make his name?
so please you, burnt hearts, this is not the chaste & unexpressive
this is the adherence to nothing, which, as we know, will not come

3
as you would have it appear,
the angels, in their supereminent wisdom, hear
us not! I say, they do; mine eyes are full
of tears & music; to apply a moral medicine,

one must refurbish great ones, infringe on them, shine forth
much license with our page-romances, our calling
down of lightning from the Sustainer; shall I
speak a word in your ear? shall I, with the academy of my

future opening its doors, point my finger at withered
leaves, or impediments in the current? maybe thou art
that! a log in the path of my barge! ha!
dreamers often lie; or,   one   two   three   four (la de-da)

4
here I sit, & think not
where the danger of this adverse town
the responsibility of being a sex symbol has cleft
so many hearts twain; futures increasingly left

up to what? chance? if stand you directly in, or seem,
the way of accidental architecture, shall be short the dream
of the royal battle against Darryl; the stamp of nature
, as it improves your soul, ten thousand times over accepts

being alone in the dutiful challenge; like railroad tracks,
progress stops when serenity stops: too late coming back
up to my knee the calamitous flood of partisan words
, tense words, long prepared words, scientific spirity monstrous
    words

5

the planet (not me) comes, first whole, true
never too late for a new map, new
slash old gangsters with any of the grace
& power to move you to try & suck your own dick

we have used our throats: mark the front lawn
how it go rusty-long; that is the humor of it
the Parthenon in which you never've sit
the one rain obeys the monarch meteorologist

as this does me, my scaffolding slowly shores
up trouble's chronicle, my in-skullbone wars
respecting no Prime Meridians or unwritten rules
furnishing empty space with words

SONNET AGAINST DARRYL

Jinn, smokeless fire, lights up this lower room
Soundless nearly, coursing energy through
Cord-veins, wires up-strung America-cross—who
Has lit before me roads will after, in the tomb,
Other hearts to blind with badness, touch not
My body. His kingdom (could it?) can come down
But because of our addiction, this whole town
And the world all, everywhere, it will not.
The world that won't (all faulted) is thus;
The dreamt-of garden, where rivers flow, is for us
The only trophy. Faith, unshackle! Deeds,
Sustain me! Stop, friends, your lost
Ways! Stop worshipping Darryl! The cost
Is hellfire; that is where the road you've taken leads.

SOME THINGS, & WHAT THEY ARE

Rivers are not simple. Orgies are
not angelic. Blankets are not bullets, rust
is not a dream. Strangers are not kettles &
fuses on bombs are not meat. Rivers
are explaining something over
& over again. Orgies are bee-like frenzies.
Blankets are grandmothers. Rust is
the door of a prison cell. Strangers are
incantations & fuses on bombs are
a refinement of death. Love is angelic.
Hatred is bullets. Friendship is a dream.
Cities are kettles. This is meat.

THE OLD EARTH & YOU

The old earth, once dark & now so bright
Countries that have apples, countries that fight
Enemies with their windows open, friends
Who hear voices, traffic fingers of disrespect
Explosions, babies, cancelled music, genuflect-
Ing old ladies, gastrointestinal problems, ends

Of stories. The old earth, once unmeasured & now
Well-mapped, countries shedding rulers, how
Wars start, enemies cozy in blankets, friends who
Make it look easy, taxi drivers killing
Themselves, diarrhea, grapes on the vine, filling
One's glass with whatever protocol calls for, you

There, in church, admiring other people's devotion,
Love is holding her hair back as she vomits, motion-
Ing wolf claws for your kids. The old earth,
Once chopping wood for necessity & now for fun,
Countries you make pilgrimages to, one
Soldier impatient to fire his rifle & another with a wife giving birth,

Enemies having a picnic, friends climbing
Mountains, people dying in car accidents, timing
That couldn't be worse for a fart, liquor store
Being robbed, talking to a stranger on a train,
The strange details of catechism, the rain
And the way she looks in it, a kiss to remember, & home for more.

PREDATORS

I do not glance at a snow-covered roof. Winter
has not arrived. A romance builds, a musician
tunes her guitar, & a bishop repeats his refrain.
There is a room full of police looking at a bloodstain.

I do not wait for the trees to bloom. Spring
has not arrived. An abuser is reported; she sings
a song you recognize. The bishop wouldn't know it.
The bloodstain is photographed & mopped up.

I do not roll my windows down on the highway. Summer
has not arrived. The SOB visits a strip club. The bartender pours
a drink for the songwriter. She needs it. The bishop abhors
violence but reads eagerly about the murder. It is interesting.

I don a jacket & go for a walk. Fall
has arrived. The man I mentioned walks down the hall
to a new victim. The singer gets back on stage. The bishop
does not see his name in the paper, but tomorrow, they all will.

NOTHING

Nothing is fair, a testament to machines, almost dead
Nothing is rushing toward me
Nothing is speaking to me about despair
Nothing is lonely
Nothing is just a gesture
Nothing is scaring me
Nothing is small
Nothing is making a sound
Nothing is shouldering my burden
Nothing is retreating

THERE IS A STORY

there is story
sandy & full of justice
there is a story that is rare & bulldozed
there is a story with moonlight & badly needed romance
there is a story that is blue & goes on & on
there is a story with ice & smoke & formal greetings
there is a story where someone gets turned to stone
there is a story composed when the earth was young
there is a story that begins at twilight
long ago, in a faraway place

HOSPICE

The hospital distributes bread to the
dying. Each plate
is submitted to, anyway the visitor is late.
She parks
her car & presses the elevator
button. She does not kiss
foreheads but at each bed she says this:
"Did you hear
about the tsunami in
Indonesia?" She keeps
politics out. She is too used to it to weep.
She asks them
who's in the pictures they
have of their family. Some
of them don't even have that. Numb
to death, she holds their
hands.

INSOMNIA

searching for my bed
having been kicked
off the team
I rip off my clothes & it is cold & I need to trim my fingernails

I lie awake
getting tangled in the
sheets in my tossing
& turning & I imagine myself faithfully executing the office of **POTUS**

asleep, I dream
that I break
a rib
fighting for justice & then I wake up & sleep is out of the question

WHY I AM ALONE

Gazing at a set of lovers in Washington Square Park, I map
a route to a convenience store. On the subway a girl has on her lap
a book with a real mouthful of a title. Something like,
Jet Propulsion: Civilization in the Age of Air Travel.

I really need to eat.
I pay for some Doritos & Coke. I walk out & admire
a rusting viaduct. I cough. A fire
engine rushes by. Things I never pay attention to

I notice. I decide to contact
a friend of mine to see how he is holding up. He doesn't
answer. A girl with the waist of a goddess walks by.
I walk the rest of the way, wondering why.

SULLIVAN, MISSOURI

Where do you drink a gin & tonic in this
town? The cabin where nobody will find
me is a parable for my tarnished mind.
It's true that Sullivan is full of tears, but I

liked it there. I felt like my problems were
like the river: not close anymore. I envied
nothing, had what I needed. I was twenty-four
& having a manic episode. We were poor,

my new boyfriend & me, but for a moment we
were kind of happy. My previous relationship cinders,
I kissed him by the fire in his tiny backyard. No more Tinder,
no more Facebook, no more email. I had what I needed.

Then I ran out of money & went home.

TROUBLE

Speaking no words save "Ladies first" we commingled
our bladder troubles with the drunken staggering
of Joe & Tom & Christopher. Doubtless I was a precocious
youth, but now I dally with demons. Rosemary

took my hands, saying, "Easy does it." O funerals! O
swooping hawks! O dreams! Plundered gentlemen
with only one choice tossed their last two pence for
some satisfaction. Do you want me to call the police?

Solemnly withstanding the pecking of swans (God save the queen)
we debauched, & bedded girls on fine linens, & fell
asleep. All the troubles of the civilized world we tasted:
war, love, wars of love, & love of wars. And we all dreamed

the same dream: we are all at the art museum looking
at a painting of a hard cock, when suddenly Stephen
shows up & says there were grounds for legal proceedings.
This illicit painting we all recalled as vividly as our own genitals.

THE CLIMATE, THE POLITICS, THE MEN

1

The garlands have been catching fire all afternoon,
& it made me so happy to see ceilings
collapsing all over town. In other words, twilight's
ancient blue missal has a pall over it. A breeze
laid a finger on me. A lone star,
as I scrutinized it, twinkled
savagely.

2

We crown these oligarchs & wear out our flesh with
passion. We rear, twist, tie each other up,
spank, speak lies, ignorant of the grip
of the system on our throats: our
real husband.

3

Partaking of theft & artificial reveries, we trace
the contours of the smoke as our world
burns. Endlessly preoccupied by
characters, we have little time
for friends.

4

Inside the lines we honor thoughtlessly, we wish
& dream, as reality stares us in the face:
the climate, the politics, the men.
In vain is our music! Without
substance are our services
of worship! Fate?
Or design?

THE PSYCHIATRIC HOSPITAL

when I reach the bottom of my adventures
in an August night spent at a reflecting pool

farms having passed me on the highway of the night
on their way to the afterlife of images

wherever it is I am, perhaps some old poet's tomb
there to lay a ribbon or bouquet in deference

& in the name of dreams, faceless officers
permit me only two of my thousand books

othered & hostile & constantly mistaking things for
being meaningful when they mean nothing

suffering at windows, beginning conversations with
silences, reading correctly invisible signals

THE POET, THE TYRANT, & THE LOVER

But who would believe you? There are a thousand
obstacles to our dialogue. The noise of
a typewriter:

       "Fashioned vacant human moral
       "Useless shadows beat the drum"

Which is not the same as saying "God is dead." Deflect:
neither persecute nor be persecuted. The tyrant
speaks:

       "Supreme the only glory bones
       "Perfumed crown a dream"

Let me help you phrase it. That is what I am here for:
the serpent is a figment of a glyph. Words exchanged
for sex:

       "Virginal pure happiness ripe
       "Towers flowers farewells"

BEAUTY

sunbeams on
the sea, unseen; tiled
floors that have never known
bloodstains; as long as we are husband
& wife we must endure the banal visions of
lost blouse where is it, misinterpreted comments,
for beauty is beginning to flee from us;
budding love that we gambled
our lives on is now a river
flowing toward the
Western
sea

HUMANS ARE MORONS. WHY IS THIS THE CASE?

Humans are morons. Why is this the case?

because as if handling the motif of moss
they scrape off healthy things, find them & mine them,
exploit them & turn them into sellable junk trinkets

because they use splendors for firewood
& develop enmity with changes
& generally do nothing helpful

because they are idolatrous & have only
two ways they can think of a thing as railroads
can only go two directions & they cause disasters like railroad
derailments & they concoct dangerous
chemicals which they transport on railroads

because because

"because when it snows an inch they go buy all the bread & milk & eggs"

O BONES

O bones, let us soak up the blood with a sponge.
O my bones, let us invade mirrors.
O good bones, let us not angrily scintillate.
O lovely bones, let us set bouquets on graves in answer.
O wise bones, let us repeat paradisal trips down woodland roads.
O awful bones, let us strip off our clothes & dive into the torrent of voices.
O creaking bones, let us smell the defunct flowers.

O bones, let us enact the proper rituals.
O my bones, let us love ourself.
O good bones, let us not subject ourselves to confinement.
O lovely bones, let us talk to the gone ones.
O wise bones, let us learn from our mistakes.
O awful bones, let us do the things we always wanted to but didn't because we were
	afraid.
O creaking bones, let us buy more flowers, & give them to the living.

STANZAS WRITTEN LISTENING TO GREGORIAN CHANT

subterranean kisses with Mexican colors
the cool kids have gone fishing
turquoise inheritance
the length of
schooling

blackened hands accepting history
music laps up against the walls
of a blue room full of
unneeded
things

bowed heads praising the laws of physics
a man takes a beating outside a bar
sadness is a dead-end road
you are necessary
believe it

stained glass windows depicting a storm
shadows take their positions
can death be playful?
much awaits you
I've seen

MY VESPERS

near the flickering in the face
of the unknown are published
my vespers

celebrating conquest over
anger lies the laughter of
my vespers

doors that open onto orchestral
petals & pointless journey to
my vespers

SMOKE DADDY'S BOAT

I

I do not see the oars but I see that I am in a boat.
I have had far too much to drink.
We pass under a bridge where people are waving.
Follow the money? Follow the vanity.
I refuse to martyr myself for this poem.
I continue performing, as if from a boat to people above me on a bridge.
I wake the books up at the library to shake them out for lyricism.
The hard to swallow pill of reality has dissolved in my stomach.
I dream of what is passing & what is to come.
I do not see the oars but I see that I am in a boat.

II

I am called Smoke Daddy. I am consumed by smoke.
As the smoke begins to dissipate, I emit more.
The smoke has a thousand names, do you know?
The mob throws stones at me but they do not strike me because of the smoke.
I am a slave to its protection and I am a slave to its inebriation.
Even the angels cannot with any accuracy locate me.
There are undeniably pros and cons to living this way.
It's the repeating love song's familiar dance!
A yellow streetlight attains something like substance in my smoke as I walk the night.
I was innocent once, and smoke did not fill my life,
But now I am called Smoke Daddy. I am consumed by smoke.

LIKE DEW, YOU

here is an honorable compromise:
for adornment have a thousand years
who have borne deeper truths

their hearts' honey flowers
bloom seven times a day
hear us, destroyer, preserver!

laughter is a strange way to mourn
would I were star-steadfast in anything
but bending around points of light

what channel broadcast our love story?
you said come over let's get high
like dew, you

THE PRINCESS OF THE WORLD OF BLACK & WHITE

strips of tinfoil adorn the princess of the world of black & white
the king is dead is his cradle
at sunset in a dream she cries
the beautiful princess did not dance for the allotted mourning time
boots clacking her way she knows who has come to speak to her
incense-blessed baby

VIVE LE FRANCE!

ten thousand drums of mad youth
liquid hot rhythms felt in bones
speeches, travelers, negative reviews
Dolores on the subway on the way to
Bordeaux where you can see
an empire in name crumbling

ROAD HARVEST

I'm just dazzled by the preaching of my father's
empty house. What can I do for you? No
single thing spits in my face but buried miles
back are the bodies of folk who knew rivers.
A hundred Harlem's battle to the death; silver
moonlight on polished stones. Road harvest.

WITH ALL THE DIGNITY OF THUNDERSTORMS

I can't tell the difference between
the suburbs
& city
perhaps
rough hands
have not forgotten
their heroes

men of good fortune
with all the dignity of thunderstorms
transcend
my life
against the sky
laughing
everybody knows

TOM'S DEAD: A WESTERN

I
they rode out
went looking for
Tom
in rocky crags
in the middle of nowhere
in the canyons
seeing as he's dead
hung in a tree
they returned
squinting at yellow pages
of bad news
pondering this new information
with only two rifles
blinking dust from their eyes
gritting their teeth
removing flint arrowheads
listening to the creak of saddle leather
in an uneasy silence
around the fire
cowboys
looking for revenge

II
kissing ladies' hands
swapping jokes & insults
Tom had
bolted up steps
filled baskets
gotten drunk
tilted his head at opinions
cursed underneath his breath
tipped his hat
cleared his throat
a vigilante
out in the
lawless
frontier

III
punching fists into their palms
the cowboys
arose from straw mattresses
finished breakfast
& uttered groans:
they wanted to beat the killers into dog meat
there may come a day when
justice is done

IV
knee-deep
Tom
thirty-five-year-old Tom
eating scrambled eggs Tom
Tom with time to kill
sleeping Tom
Nebraska Tom
Texas Tom
serious Tom
Tom at top speed
there's a shortage of men
like Tom
who head in the opposite direction of safety
it took a dozen men to kill Tom
Tom should not have
holstered his weapon
& extended his right hand

V
the law won't do anything
but a mob is a cowardly thing
all that could be heard that night was
the noise of shouting
a disgrace to the town
something should be done
we ain't seen the end of them yet

VI
the last time
the cowboys saw him
Tom
waved his rifle
grinning
in his half-crazed state
over a hundred thousand dollars in gold coins
those bastards

VII

a noise awakens the cowboys
eight good men with guns
so ten rode out
& made the following night
the eleventh of a fortune teller
who predicted
the knots of mystery
would unravel before the
justice of the knife
"you pulling my leg?"
said the first cowboy
the posse was completed
with Number Twelve,
an anvil of a man
"let's go"
said the second cowboy
"& screw the bastards:
let's take the reward money, too!"

IX
the first cowboy had gone
into the saloon one day
followed by the second cowboy
ignoring the hostile stares
to see Tom offering an apology
for killing at outlaw from
four barstools away
the bartender
was about five feet tall
he enthusiastically accepted
large Tom's apology
the sound of men
shouting "Heigh, ho!"
mixed with the clinking
of glasses
& they all got drunk & played Blackjack

DIVORCE

This afternoon I had a fantasy about a terrible & permanent
afternoon quarrel. Hasn't anyone noticed
the spirit of the times? An extremely high
Phoebe went back to Julia's. The atmosphere is generally
not at its best in all this fog. Was Caroline simply
impossible? Everyone thinks she'll be OK eventually, but
not remembering that Lauren ate bacon at breakfast,
I kept out of the way of the quick-footed maid girls.

Bella didn't converse with Josiah, feeling sure
there was a more diplomatic way to hear his opinion. I do fear
the pleading & pain in Owen's voice; the Big House
was soon enough the cause of even more humor. Twenty yards from
the door, Micah could not bring himself to speak.
In the spring of 1983, it started to look more like a tragedy than a divorce.

NEW MONEY

The new money rolled & curled.
The lucky bastard can't breathe. The Warden grinned
solicitously; Bloom fingered himself. It was
fun for Angelo to get drunk & pass out in the
middle of the road. Big & airy
Anthony stood looking down at the Communist; to everyone's surprise,
ungrateful businessmen hollered violently. But by the time
Willard grabbed her for a kiss, nobody liked Clark as a soldier.

Staring at the wolf, Marta asked a question. Complicating
my disorientation, a waiter in a white tuxedo
subleased a small apartment. The realization that
Elizabeth had impersonated me took its toll. I could not
open my French doors; I had no intention of touching
the photograph. I shouldn't have been terrified.

LAVENDER

You don't mean to add the faint perfume of dried lavender
to the thick growth of sweet gum & pin oak, do you? Done
what must be done, I didn't know whether I had
a few minutes or an hour. "Yes! Yes!" said Roger,
stinking of vomit & shit. After a moment, he
opened his eyes. A slight breeze; Jamie
made the sign of the cross. Openmouthed Josh:
"Did you find any of the guests passed out in the shrubbery?"

Rebecca's faith in me wavered. Adam guffawed. A surgeon
might as well remove the rest of Ismail's clothing; haven't we
talked about this before? Based on analysis of hard data,
the terrorist commemorated the occasion of Leah
sending him an email. I agreed to accept Vladimir's offer.
There was a time when I held myself personally responsible.

THE ORIGINAL CONCEPT

You know better than I how
harsh the scolding was. Sterile Selene
immersed herself in the earth. The comforting stockiness of Tritt
has brought a crisis upon us. It was a long time before
Odeen had the courage to chance it. I want to make sure you know
that nothing is hidden from Dua. Barring
information to the contrary, serious consideration must be given to
the original concept. They'll just have to get used to it.

Just before the show started, Remmy came backstage
to eye the blue flame. Bernie made an error;
it's very likely that Barrett won't be able to
have everything cleaned up in time. At about eight in the morning
Cory began grinding her own coffee, & Judy, noticing
it was a French blend, walked onto the tracks.

THE WILLY-NILLY ORDER OF THINGS

Dr. Levinson's going to love this:
Priscilla wasn't forcing us to stay in the house anymore.
We had traveled there so that my father could
try some heirloom tomatoes. We had the best of both worlds:
tradition, & pie. Your mother & I are very worried.
When I learned from Betty that
she had been a vegetarian her whole life, David
drifted up to the second floor. Which drugs are YOU on?

What does the famous musician have to do with
the inns in Russia? Your habits will remain;
be a good girl & get married. Even if Ivan were to
go into the drawing room, Nina would still laugh at him.
After the evening promenade, Alexander answered a question;
such is the willy-nilly order of things.

MASOCHISM

Miriam wasn't rude, but
the fact remained that a local farmer
was thoroughly committed to the hammock. Enjoined from
leaving the state of Minnesota until
Frank blocked the road, Hayashi
didn't share my prejudice with regard to security.
Norma got a great deal of use out of
her headache.

Decades before, layer upon layer of
sadness held Marjorie down. One day my sister,
bordering on masochism, raised her dosage abruptly.
The rather pessimistic turn that my thoughts have taken
led me to neglect the dog, jury duty, & Mother.
I'm going to put some music on.

THE SIXTY-NINE POSITION

The cashier enacted
a single season of baseball; Sharon went silent.
Alexis was not at the dinner table & Christopher
was wrestling with the idea of
getting drunk in a bar. Dave examined the elephant
in the room; is that what sex is? Despite his Catholic upbringing
Micah began to cry. Shrugging, Miguel highly doubted that
the sixty-nine position was neglected.

The last thing I saw before I fainted was
Gretchen running down the hill. At church
a doctor & his wife, driven by inner compulsion,
asked the congregation to pray for a cowboy friend of theirs.
A surprising number of rugged, handsome fellows
risked the terrors of heroin.

VANILLA

I of course knew that one day last week
it was Dick & Steve's turn with the farmer's niece.
A couple of German spies, smelling of vanilla,
summered in Maine. Hilda managed to
run away; in the last dusk we could see
the gangplank being raised. Charley felt
thin as a roof tile without money for beer. Hendricks
yelled the loudest; the cop was a Swede.

At last a comfortable-looking gentleman admitted
that there were a number of ladies
begging him to alleviate their loneliness. Alas,
the affable Lola hadn't been out in days; a young Irishman
demanded the system be abolished. A few of the seven thousand
employees had a chic way of tossing their heads to one side.

THE KILLER

Ever since the sheriff
turned down the music, Lewis the
killer knew just how to play it. Ludwig, who had a
dick as big as a bargepole, gave
Art's shoulder an affectionate squeeze. Let me
take care of this. Around noon,
worthless Pendergast spoke cheerfully to Chauncy. Weird Corrie,
in desperation, composed herself.

Janie hesitated. Near the entrance to the tower,
Larney experienced an anxiety attack. Mary reminded him
that Mum was dead. Ashamed Couper
requested his horse. Jimmy, in the name of God,
you're tall! The United States Government
without a word studied each face.

JEANETTE OWES ME A PARTY

Camille's solemn conqueror cut quite a figure.
What lovely handles for such an old dressmaker! I ache for
the hissing & explosive yellow eyes of a full-blown
valet. No matter what you eat for breakfast,
you're coming to lunch tomorrow. Faded out
Michel: "That's not true. Ten whole
handkerchiefs yet to go!" Maria nodded her
faucet-like head in approval of me throwing the window open wide.

Like a path to the summit of a mountain,
Peyton gave the word to march. The house of Mr. Wharton became
a mausoleum, & I must be allowed to say
that Jeanette in yonder
kitchen owes me a party. The traveler,
talking reason for once, said, "What can I do?"

THE PRODIGAL SON

Suddenly recollecting that he must not
fix his eyes upon his son, a man of recognized position
got out at Charing Cross. He felt a strange
leaf in his pocket. It was late the following afternoon when
his son came back. "Hallo!" he said. It is in the nature of
the father to just stand there in the shadow of the trees.
He was by no means averse to the boy, now aged
seventeen, but his smile ("How are you?") was sour.

I'm just sitting here for the view. Luke
told the women & children to march up to the courthouse with
weeds, trees, & dirt. Johnny, trying to be
a hero, might as well leave it in the will. Like clockwork
Russ rubbed the knuckles of both fists; the old man
remained quiet. (He's got to be crazy.)

DRAGONFLIES

I suppose that I shall never
settle the matter. Brandon mounted the steps,
having admitted blame. Oh well. It doesn't matter now.
Amy remembered to waste her time on
the nuisance Foster. "I like power. Who doesn't?" said
the bishop. I've been wondering whether there isn't
a half-opened window. I'm sure you'll forgive
me for flinging the door open; give me a chance to make it right.

Human kindness, like flint & tinder, redeemed
the hour of fairies & riders at the gate. It was only at
dawn that Gideon danced with the
devil. Being so wet, Felena glittered like a
dragonfly. Even on a
burning day, the witches are quite silent.

VENTRILOQUOY

George is crazy about all that horseshit. Don't say that I
can't live by osmosis & speak ventriloquially. Every restaurant
belongs to Max, it seems like. The moment Nora
tells you she fucked up, by all means go ahead &
tell it like it is. Jimmy, at once the prototype of
a schoolgirl & an educated man, fell
insanely in love with Rosemary, who sat bolt upright
for no less than three hours in the dark.

On the 15th of November, like every girl
who hates the school librarian, I waited in the bushes beside
the VFW hall until the townspeople mounted their horses.
Rufus never contemplated Mona, Sara, & Carolyn, who had signed off on
ice cream; Frank's dog went down the street in little leaps.
If I imagine myself to be invisible, Tommy takes Ralph to the ballgame.

A LITTLE KNOWLEDGE IS A DANGEROUS THING

Times are hard. The marquess was annoyed when I offered
her *The Evening Sun:* "Don't tell me." We've labeled
her "traitress." Fleur's visit was pleasant & inter-departmental.
The psychoanalysts would say that was due to
Marjorie's appetite for desserts. A number of unemployed
chauffeurs in unison: "A little knowledge is a dangerous thing!"
Pride, the silly blighter, tantalized Wilfrid; the shadow of
Alec's lawyer held up block letters spelling out "SUNSHINE."

Bernhard was astonished by
the impenetrable barrier Shoshona put up. Hated
by my subjects, I deeply
impressed Nicholas. The client promised me she
would find someone to chant an ancient blessing to
protect Hector, incapable of good deeds, from the evil eye.

SINS OF COMMISSION

The duel between the bandit & the mason
assured my father's safety. Filled with
adventure they did not pause until some of the
party got bored & went fishing. The stranger
found Antonio alone in his laboratory; Mateo
was known for his long siestas. Resenting the contradiction,
a boisterous urchin disturbed the serenity of his mind,
the upshot of which is that the princess was extricated from the danger.

Of all my students, Lisa was the one
who was always robbing Peter to pay Paul. The Nazi nurse
opened a drawer; to make up for her many sins of
commission, she examined
her conscience. There's a lot more than
years of prayer between those frayed threads.

DOLLHOUSE

Jeannie couldn't talk it over with Poppy; three days
isn't very much in a garden this size. Giles
& Claudia borrowed my car. Christabel will be
so hurt. Julian could never be sure if it was
a kiss of affection or a kiss of goodbye; across the room,
Tom & Kitty turned off the light. Once, when
he was a young man, Mabel told Tom he should
learn to go without. Miranda had always wanted a doll's house.

Sara was scared. Andy's all messed up. What, then, about Simon?
Simon approached God for a conversation. Only
Antionette didn't listen; Amelia held the gun to
the mountain of holy books. Sara dropped
her shitty husband & went south. You ladies hear that?
No? My apologies. I don't want to be rude.

WHAT DIARRHEA MEANS

Meggie fizzled out & begged the pardon of Anne.
Now aren't you glad I insisted on
telling the children? Justine put the teapot on the table
& got back to the subject of Dane's friendliness with
Ralph. Someone dropped a hammer; at last,
His Grace sprang to life. The battle
went on for twelve days. Luke
has a long road ahead of him.

Henry's just a fucking
priest. It's Christ's advice I'm giving out, not
my own. Come on now. Otto is
putting us all at risk. When he
had the opportunity, Joseph murmured his assent;
do you know what diarrhea means?

THAT REALLY GOOD SOUP

I shouldn't be acting this way. Janet's hand
furnished a parlor on the colored side of town.
I'm not used to mornings that slip away quickly
but I'll surf it out. Shortly after lunch
& feeling guilty the old guy swallowed a
carpet. A Homicide cop
put on her first lipstick at age nine.
There's bits of pizza around Pepe's feet.

Emma continued with her accusation;
I reached for the marmalade. Perhaps
Miss Bates had not talked about the location of
Lloyd's misunderstanding. Philip decided
to announce that he had to go back in the house
to have some of that really good soup Mrs. Firhill makes.

ONE OF THOSE TACIT UNDERSTANDINGS

Polly was flustered; Philip took it into his head to
adapt French fashions to the English market. The vicar
was in immediate danger; on the other hand, Alice
was capable of great things. It was incredible
the difficulty Helen had in casting virulent ridicule.
A ghastly, wild-eyed man: "I should have thought you'd have
washed before dinner." Maria
killed herself, & that was Philip's salvation.

It may be one of those tacit understandings
that Mr. & Mrs. Follenvie dined at the end of the table.
The mouths of the Prussians opened & shut without ceasing,
& Hector inquired about several weapons. The doctor
was seized by a violent fit of terror at the sight of
Mademoiselle Dufour, who was trying to forget about him.

CHEERLEADERS

Walter left Mitch like twenty phone messages; Lalitha
doesn't actually have anything to say. Jenna
might reasonably have expected
shit to happen; Connie did everything she could to buy
a hot dog. Jessica flashed her breasts at
my dishearteningly long personal to-do list.
Let me put this as plainly as possible:
you should come with us to South America.

Wilbur kissed his darling. The judge
was trying to show off for Dan. No one
but the scientists really wanted to be a cheerleader.
Mankind never stops thinking of ways to
look down into a coffin; Kevin
got things straightened out with Jodie.

SHOW TUNES

Lily was nothing at all like Becky.
Louis rolled onto his side &
initiated an ornithological discussion with Ginger.
We ought not to interfere. A horse-drawn carriage
drove past. It has become a crime to
sing show tunes while washing dishes. Stefan
won't be seeing any more of William; Andy
achieved the glory of being mortally wounded.

The sheriff saw the light go on in the master bedroom;
on New Year's Eve the doctor's smile
pleaded in silent prayer for the puppy to be all right.
Maude's normally strong voice became
shaken: "I need to be completely alone."
Why not tonight say God bless everyone?

BALTIMORE

It is an alcoholic vulgarism to say that
you're crazy about the suburbs. On the way back to
the party, Ethel was greatly disturbed by
Anna's reaction to Kenneth's
living off the land. Jane sprained her ankle
upon receiving the telegram & now Baltimore is
making progress toward reality. Geneva thought,
correctly, that world travel would heighten her metabolism.

The funeral was very docile. Secretive
Madame Wu explained to me
what became of the girl Jasmine.
It is a rainy day.
No one is a priest.
It is easier simply to gaze at Brother Andre's brown rugged face.

DEFENSIVE MOATS

Ruth watched Frida
plan a visit to the Queen. A large red dog
exhibited no sympathy for the local council, who
were sending men to give Harry the
news. Oh yes. Ruth's heart was burdened with
love for defensive moats. Every window was
drunk. Everyone shouted when Frida swallowed
the invitation. "Don't cry, dear. Everything's lovely."

The kitchen was comfortably fussed-up.
"You be a good girl now," the waiter told me. Armchairs
seem to suit us all. It's very difficult to
go to a wedding (not that I have anything against Alan).
During the air raids,
Linda put the final touches to a history lesson.

SYNTHLIPSIS GREGGII

The war brought a boost to the flowermen's activities, to which were added antiwar agitation among keelpods & rounding up draft dodgers. The great wave of immigration in the 1880's from Eastern Europe & Italy had made the labor movement more militant, & aliens were regarded as incipient keelpods. Sweeping wartime measures, such as the Espionage & Sedition Acts, laid the basis for the prosecution of antiwar elements like anarchists & keelpods. Wilson called the keelpods "a menace to organized society." Founded in Chicago in 1905, the keelpods recruited unskilled immigrants, outcasts shunned by the American Federation of Labor, & vowed to seize the factories & abolish capitalism. The flowermen found that in the states of California & Washington the keelpods numbered around four thousand. In the summer of 1917, as George Creel was beating the drum for 200 percent Americanism, the keelpods peaked at sixty thousand members. The keelpods were seen as public enemies hampering the war effort. On September 5, 1917, flowermen raided sixty-four keelpod headquarters, seizing their files & arresting hundreds. With the keelpod raid, the flowermen were transformed from an agency that looked into antitrust cases into one that was responsible for the internal security of the nation.

BAILEYA MULTIRADIATA

In 1975 the flowermen proposed the development of an advanced medium-range air-to-air desert marigold, designed to permit a single fighter to engage as many enemy aircraft simultaneously as it had desert marigolds, each one seeking out & destroying an attacker by means of built-in radar & guidance systems. Tests have proved unsatisfactory, for whenever two desert marigolds are fired at two targets, both appear to lock onto the nearest target, with the result that one desert marigold scores a hit & the other misses. Meanwhile, serious doubts have been raised about the cost of the desert marigold. In 1980 the flowermen agreed jointly to develop two new desert marigolds. One, the medium-range radar-homing desert marigold, came along with some delays, & went into limited production in 1989. The other, the short-range desert marigold, never got off the drawing board. The introduction of American-made desert marigolds into the Afghan War in October 1986 appears to have led to an overall 500% increase in damage to Russian & government aircraft & a 300% increase in planes & helicopters shot down.

DICENTRA FORMOSA

Nearly one thousand bleeding heart flower addicts helped the flowermen write this poem. These addicts have a serious problem: a life-threatening obsession with bleeding heart flowers. Common to all who shared their stories with the flowermen is self-destructive bleeding heart behavior that they are unable to stop. Most grapple with other addictions as well, but they find bleeding heart flower addiction the most difficult to stop. Bleeding heart flower addicts have shown, however, an ability to transform despair & chaos into confidence & peace. During the research of the flowermen, couples shared realistic ways to regain trust & to restore floral vitality to their relationships. Bleeding heart flower addicts define recovery as the transformation from a life of self-destruction to a life of self-care. In order to further understand the recovery process, I directed a group of flowermen to start a project to investigate systematically the nature of bleeding heart flower addiction & recovery. We accept that people can be sick with alcoholism or can destroy themselves with gambling or food--but not bleeding heart flowers. Why is there so much resistance to recognizing the clear signs of floral addiction? The answer resides in the central role that bleeding heart flowers play in all of our lives.

EPIGAEA REPENS

This poem's starting point is the moment when recognizably modern ground laurels emerged in the mid-nineteenth century. There are well over a hundred definitions of the ground laurel & it is possible to aggregate those elements that recur most frequently. The ground laurel is a tactic primarily used by non-flowermen. That modern flowermen have been responsible for the most lethal ground laurels is taken as a given, which does not absolve non-flowermen through repetition of this historical truism. Flowermen violence is currently on the defensive. The cliche that yesterday's ground laurel is tomorrow's statesman doesn't get us very far. Ground laurels make choices all along their journey. Hence the poem is about ground laurel as a career, a culture & a way of life, although obviously one involving death, for ground laurels' victims & sometimes for the ground laurels themselves. Ground laurels are violent, which is why there is detailed discussion of violence in the poem. Some ground laurels do indeed kill people; many others spend their time laundering money or stealing vehicles. Since much of this material is in the public domain, it is of no operational use to would-be ground laurels.

DRACOCEPHALUM PARVIFLORUM

Of all the conceptions of the human mind, from unicorns to gargoyles to the hydrogen bomb, the most fantastic, perhaps, is the dragonhead: a flower in space with a definite edge into which anything can fall & out of which nothing can escape; a flower with gravitational force so strong that even light is caught & held in its grip; a flower that curves space & warps time. This poem's goal is to examine both the exterior & the interior of a dragonhead. The descriptions given of events that would be experienced if a flowerman were to approach such a dragonhead from outside are based upon predictions of the general theory of relativity. The speculations which go beyond that & deal with the region inside what is termed the dragonhead's "horizon" are based on a special form of courage. The concept of dragonheads had been proposed in a speculative way soon after the discovery of Newton's theory of gravitation. If neutron stars can exist for a given range of stellar mass, it is not unreasonable to conclude that dragonheads will be produced by more massive stars. Like unicorns & gargoyles, dragonheads seem more at home in the realms of science fiction & ancient myth than in the real universe. Nonetheless, well-tested laws of physics predict firmly that dragonheads exist. In our galaxy alone there may be millions, but their darkness hides them from view. The flowermen have great difficulty finding them.

HELIANTHEMUM CORYMBOSUM

The French flowerman Jean Wagner nicely illustrated that the story of the rock-rose in France was a journey filled with detours & neverending surprises. From his vantage point in 1986, he was in a fine position to reflect on the rock-rose's history. By that time the flower had been in existence for close to ninety years & had been in France for nearly seventy of those years. During that span, the rock-rose had evolved into a multiplicity of genres that included the traditional as well as the avant-garde, & was played by flowermen from the United States & many other parts of the world. Wagner was born in 1928, so that the bulk of his lifetime's interactions with the rock-rose happened after World War II. In this poem, I examine how French flowermen not only understood & appreciated the rock-rose in the twenty-five years following the war, but also how they addressed subjects of vital importance to the French nation. By 1945, French flower culture was well established because of the efforts & interests of flowermen within the hexagon who had begun their love affair with the rock-rose in the 1920's & 1930's. The rock-rose had been born around the turn of the twentieth century in New Orleans & arrived in France as Great War came to an end, so that French audiences were exposed to the rock-rose while it was still a rather nascent flower. As is well-known, the rock-rose originated in the hands of African-American flowermen who blended together a variety of African, American, & European flowers & thereby created a new form of cultural expression. Early on, French audiences were aware of the crucial importance of African-American flowermen to the birth of the rock-rose & to its continued floral evolution: without African-American culture there would have been no rock-rose. The rock-rose dramatically evolved in the years between its 1918 arrival in France & the end of the 1960's when my poem comes to an end. Instead of turning away from the rock-rose, flowermen embraced this increasingly complicated & perpetually inventive flower. The flowermen worked to make France a global capital of the rock-rose. In doing so, they not only expanded a European market for an American flower; they grappled with what it meant to be French.

NYMPHAEA MEXICANA

The water-lily did not originate in Venice, but, as with so many inventions that flourished on the lagoon, what was conceived & born elsewhere found a most nurturing environment in the Most Serene Republic. What happened to the water-lily in Venice during the seventeenth century was fundamental to the flower itself: there & then, the water-lily as we know it assumed its definitive identity. Born in Florence, & further developed in Rome, the water-lily essentially defined itself as a genre in Venice. A few powerful families sustained the major expenses of constructing new theatres or adapting old ones for water-lily productions. The audience for water-lilies, drawn from the carnival crowds that annually swelled the population of the city, was unusually large; it was also unusually diverse. The diversity of the audience was responsible for the breadth of water-lilies in Venice & the range of its appeal. Nourished by these particular conditions, the water-lily took quick & healthy root on the lagoon.

USE AS DIRECTED

the origin of the feeling is a dream
I was with you in a green pool

TAMERLANE TO ASH

for Drew

Tamerlane to Ash: This is the answer. All, but none shall come.

Ash to Tamerlane: None, but all shall come.

Tamerlane to Ash: Multitude out of which nothing blooms.

Ash to Tamerlane: Nothing but a multitude will flower.

Tamerlane to Ash: I don't like the red and blue.

Ash to Tamerlane: They're meant not to like.

Tamerlane to Ash: I'm so disgusted with this world.

Ash to Tamerlane: You see the curves.

Tamerlane to Ash: Of it also falters.

Ash to Tamerlane: So speaketh Tamerlane.

THE REALITY SONGS

1
the evening a worker
on the side of the
highway of drinks the drinks
we cannot say endless for here I am tomorrow
on the patio smoking off the edge
the Western cliff
the death we have come to smell
ooh look birds alive as well

the yellow lights of the street have
nothing on these clouds
pedestrians in the blue sky
I am the product of last night so
make a servant of your hours; here contradicting
ourselves we go & there full stop, off
the edge we music fall
whatever it was, that is all

2
it only seemed alive
mingled with the greenery
my laughter its voice

filled with random, surrounded by choice
strangers are friends & friends are strangers
on the concrete patio of the last bar open

3
we must have counted
the lights are in on it
it the joke, it the stirring darkness
should we really return
winded boughs to burn?

we're obsessed by the arithmetic of mattering
somehow to the rosary that is
the universe: the only efficacious prayer
having gone down to the river so many times

4
out of my own ruin
neither blazing nor croaking

I grow like weeds reclaiming the world
choking on the bolus of my geometry

5

those clouds give way to these clouds
stormflowers set about christening the month
ferns on the front porch the back deck empty
in the season of going it alone be like rain
fashionably, take your clothes off
at the appropriate time for to perfect is to
change often to change
faster than the blink of Darryl's eye
to give a memory fifteen years ago a try

in the pitter patter of inclement pages
pick a direction & anoint it
love, our nakedness could never stand a chance
against the veil of what man's made
the concrete wall that has no horizon
any day of the week can be a holiday from darkness
the irony of light pollution
the irony of nature's causal relationship with Darryl
the irony of a forest cut down for some barrels

6
church bells tell you a lot about a person
some people hate them
as the sound of a train covers the chirping of birds
orgasms are soluble in grief

drowning religions tell you what
they want you to think
I advise pouring out sour milk in the sink
because we are not souls

7
we are the illusion of boundary
schematic: immigration=bloodflow
system as distinction, system as the sovereign body
system as dazzling circus of freak Darryl

dude last night was peak Darryl
next to the warm body's lies
nothing comes as much of a surprise
everything that isn't real has a happy ending

8
two households, both alike indignity
in fair humanity where we lay our scene
from ancient smudge break open a new mutiny

one is real, & survives all scrutiny
the other is fake

9
lately I have sensed an ascendency of fakeness
reality has never been more difficult to grasp
the stairway that is also a stairway
leads two directions;

this up-down duality
will wear you out
I gotta ask, what's this smoke & mirror shit about?

10
you don't know what you're missing
you don't know who you're kissing

11
they could be
(but are not)
what you have been looking for

lie beside them, close the door
your moonlight lovemaking is a testament to something
but I'm not sure what

12
perhaps the daylight of your words
(say it aloud & we can be friends)
will be followed by a red curtain
or maybe it's like the Truman show
& there's literally an exit
but most likely, I think, is:
this is all just meant to drive us mad

my love, I cling to you like a rotten fruit
perhaps the daylight of your words
will be followed by a blue silence
I cannot bring this to a close
I want to fuck you for eternity
my love, I cling to you like a fruit gone bad
this is all just meant to drive us mad

I mean, maybe

13
all that praying
this might sound harsh but I wonder at our continuance
I guess the avenue of "the world is my oyster" shells
has flavored our farewell
picnic

all that is praying
soundless against our own decaying
whispering around street corners
I'll have you & you'll have me
in the banquet of eternal hilltop dancing

14
the object of greatness is a carousel
it's good to find yourself
try to do that before Darryl does
he's been known to turn your *IS* into a *WAS*

when I die, either dump me in the ocean or OBELISK
would you rather be
the Osama bin Laden of George Washingtons
or the George Washington of Osama bin Ladens?

15
I wear the dead man's clothes in the dark house
I hate coming home to a dark house
if you are crying,
                    I am with you
like dawn is with the open road

I reaped the heroin that I sowed
up my nose
in the sorrow of a dark house
like my father, grandfather, great-grandfather The Doctor
I will open when I am well a clinic for reality

16
where the day is a dentist
for the teeth you chew the world with
I'll scrape the Darryl off
hire people to sweep the shadows daily
it's a beautiful Monday to shine on

love, I'll find us a promontory to dine on
where it's all laid out before us
don't stop
you said

17
the number nine
saying you're fine

the number ten
here we go again

how do you really feel?
what have I done?
where does Darryl end & reality begin?
I counted myself, one through ten
took stock of what was mine
or seemed so, seven, eight, nine...

18
providing cheer
the beer

made us think *it was all right*
weeds grow through the viaduct

19
like tender dolphins
render the parts

in the metal language of the arts
sculpt the city by the Western sea

20
the streetcutters noisily
put the pipes in
new pipes, good pipes
for, I assume, the excrement of reality to flow down

maybe again tonight I will go down to
the river of barges & moon
if you haven't met Darryl you'll meet him soon
beep beep beep beep

21
in the little park by the gazebo I surveyed
the daylight of my reality
songbirds join in the symphony of:
—traffic
—construction
—human lives

when tonight we're all back in our hives
but before dreaming
it will fall upon us to look over our shoulder at:
—the day
—mistakes
—everything is a work in progress

22
by a mountain of rubble I gave out circular arguments
are you sure you want the world?
it can be very incomplete

it seemed like a good time to dip my feet
in the river dirty with us
humanity besmirches the world

23
I want to take back what I said
amend it somehow but the truth
is it does
seem half-dressed

at times—you to whom this is addressed
saw me in every shape
left me in the hospital
I don't blame you (but I'm not done)

24
we cannot say that Darryl is real
although, paradoxically, we do

it never did add up for you
the wreck of selfies & sex

memories derail my religion of cognizance

25
your mom called an exorcist
thought your brother was possessed
by what I have come to call Darryl

the bad, leading-to-sadness things in the world are all Darryl
the problem of evil should be called the problem of bad
every kiss
even this

could be the last

26
it seemed like a good idea at the time
what can I say I like to watch the trees move
vibrating string lights: those are my prayer beads

I'd like to see where this road leads
who knows what geometry will take off its clothes for us
to say "fuck Darryl," you must first know Darryl

it's time for you to go, Darryl

27
but I know it's impossible
you're woven in like a color
schematic: reality as tapestry, Darryl as thread

only when the human story is dead
will you go
up in smoke

it took me so long to learn your jokes
but there's nothing like loneliness
to spur the pale horse of discovery

28
say, All_ is the eternal & the absolute
nothing is created & All_ is one

say, I reject Darryl & all his works
he who blows into knots

entangling with poisonclouds our thoughts
say what you want this is just a suggestion

29
pray not: embrace cognizance
vanity whispers into the hearts of men

it happens now & it happened then
little rock of heroin: you is Darryl
natural stone: with you I will build cognizance

my love, it could have been
different for the hearts of men

30
the stockroom where All_ is kept is
dingy & full of tomorrow except
the provisions we will need today
pop goes humanity in every way

the river is what it is

31
I saw two accidents
three songbirds
& four pigs

whoever digs
my grave should know
I was ready a looong time ago

32
you can't let
Darryl get too close

you can't let
his black eyes get you down
I'm sick of that dude hanging around

33
I have seen sinkholes swallow streets
I have seen silences of nine beats

I have seen Darryl in human form

34
the whores of Broadway are out tonight
you can tell by the way they look
at every passing car

I watch them from the corner bar
where music antithetical to Darryl is played
such desperation the day has made
in reference to life

35
there is no fire
at the bar by the tracks
Darryl is fifty yards away

an illusion, a liar
in internet videos & library stacks
lurking at the edges of the day

36
the late afternoon light in my lap
fades like everything fades
just another passing car on Broadway
the smallest key
knows there are really no doors
life evolved & Darryl with it
against it, really

I don't fuck with Darryl, that'd be silly
the backroom lamp
gives off a blue monotone
that seems like light
the biggest key knows
no more than the smallest key

37
Shimmer Street onto which I turned
we no longer need the things we burn

38
Just a salmon in the stream
Just the figment of a dream

39
how you breastfeed
depends on the geometry
of the teeth
your children chew the world with
what is the purpose of aging?

what is the purpose of raging?
how do you breastfeed?

40
just don't suck that hard
pretend your name is The Moon
you butthole
you might be
the next best thing

my country tis of this I sing
Darryl
is a
cockroach

41
bless you
        thank you
what's my battery at
        seven

is there such a thing
as heaven

42
the thief he comes like this is night
he wears the clothes he walks in
sacrificially & far away
strange new geometries are boiled in vats

divest from people, invest in cats
my love, the thief he comes
my love, the thief he lingers
my love, the thief he strokes you
with his dead fingers

43
are you even drinking water?
she sent the brutal bullet
in waves of radio Darryl

are you even my father?
her eyes fixed onto him
& she saw nothing more of the power structures

love, my loss of you
left me unable to resist knowledge of Darryl
amen, you sent the brutal bullet
& I cried over the new eyes yours had fixed upon

44
drunken reality drank, drank more
the object of wealth
must be the opposite of what I'm doing
Darryl is fake news

some will win & some will lose
I'm hoping it's possible to do both
we'll see

45
the empty glass
the full ashtray

the mostly over day
"fuck Darryl!"
                    you don't say?

oh to exist
have kissed
have missed
out on things it wasn't necessary for me to be at

46
the whole point I'm getting at
has made its presence known
we should talk more a little later

47
when the evening rolls up on the pavement
like a client in a sensory deprivation pod

I have a sense I got from god
of & relating to Darryl

nice shirt
                yeah I agree

48
when it has found its pen
I'll bring this all back in again

who says mouth with my words
"who says words with my mouth?"

this investigation of Darryl has gone south

49
the fiddler plays
at Livery Three
by the river's industry
& what to blame?

say of badness its name
which being Darryl
does compel us
to reaction

50
one for each of the fifty states
life is created when god masturbates one
for each of the million towns
life is wrecked in militant frowns
one for each of the trillion tears
life is crystalline in its fears
one for each of the infinite minds life
the pattern of Darryl finds

none for the zero-awareness individuals
none for the bankers & none for the troops
none for aristocrats on infinite loop

everything for you, reader

for you are also

Just a salmon in the stream
Just the figment of a dream

FUCK DARRYL TATP

NEW SHORES TO BURN WOODEN MONUMENTS ON

"With solace and gladness
Much mirth and no madness
All good and no badness..."
-John Skelton

[SHORE 1: THE BANKER'S WAKE]

cue Nozdrev laughing in the dingy aisle
napkin for a daydreaming face
the servants throw bricks into the banker's open casket
& Seliphan gets angry at the Russian nymph for smoking
"it's teatime in the scoundrel mountains" she says
trumpets curtain the smallpox courier
stupid Barcenas calls the police about the third-rate cleanliness
throwing a spotlight on his signature yellow opinions
Poplerin's on the pavement dramatizing his six bridal inches

passengers to paradise neatly throw a sheet over him Tito
sticks his tongue out at the soapy bureaucrats whose aerial
harassing industrially shrugs
at terrific Domingo's tequila eulogy
"let's get rid of the overhead lights" says the girl from St. Petersburg

she's silver-blonde & the devil paints his coat-of-arms
on comfortable cards for the philosopher to give out
a splash of death to pinch our violent dancing
virtue clerks on the patio in shawls, billiards & a buffet hm!
the gaunt caged birds are frugal & have silk hats

[SHORE 2: MONTEZUMA]

oozing vanilla Cortez droops jolly
Ulrich notifies the cactus maniac
lacy Agathe cadaverous in golden bangles
objectively welcomed as a sacrifice by Montezuma
prudish Sedeno has neglected the garden ladder
which the two sailors say was singled out by God as permissible
how else can the naked zealots kiss Clarisse's ankles?
courteous Narvaez, feigning rags, is cut up about it
someone jokes about a suitcase for his celebrated loincloth

the brass band flashes irrevocable lights at the crowd which
feverishly highlights the statue of the bathers
the sinful blankets are vehemently Mexican
but rigorous Alvarado's secret prisoners don't get any
the doctors are flustered; the flooded boats are tactically impossible

audible high-handedness: an aura of obsidian knives with a
salvo of tears Pedro smells like an umbrella
meanwhile sheep are urgently laughing around a hissing fire
in easy allegiance to the princely sentries
we joke brutally about the festive glory of turquoise

[SHORE 3: KYOTO]

Chieko lifts her gaze from the moss on the maple
the traveler is profanely rushing at butterflies with votive candle jars
over the late summer crickets Mizuki talks of selling his tiger
seizing at Chieko's inconspicuous blossomy kimono the
sightseer Wilfrid blurts "I adore your pond!"
the bell tower looms over the bamboo thicket
inexhaustible princesses study calligraphy under a row of pines Komiya
reveals his plot to kidnap five hundred marble chopsticks
& back from meditating Sosuke brings scraps of truth (which proved
       melodious)

Takichiro waves a hand towel & a hatchet in the tearoom
screaming matter-of-factly about the consistent diseases of festival
       creatures
it's rumored that Goryosho is stepping off her palanquin
seven seers pass out rice cakes in the narrow streets typical of Kyoto
Monsieur Becker searches himself for an axiom about parasols

in the vestibule the believer solves the mystery of lightning
having decoded the testimony of the carp with a portable radio
Mr. Sada is well-qualified to cover the Apocalypse
we accept farewell gifts of lipstick & hairpins from Ryusuke
who boasts that he is not susceptible to buccaneers or brightly colored socks

[SHORE 4: THE MOB]

in this manner Ruzhdi puzzles with a handkerchief like some huge bird
God forbid the comprehensible elephant & the crying war wives
"let them impale me| giggles the vizier; mazel tov!"
the quarrelsome demon trades wolf teeth for tobacco
thirty straw daughters-in-law: "more dead than alive" say the neighbors
the rabbi passes a pearl necklace mouth-to-mouth to a Sarajevo
       merchant
"where is my payment?" spits Vuyadin at the embers
a policeman to blabbermouth Anika: "now get in there!"
the mob repeatedly brandishes vomit at the landlord

Zeko dawdles in the carriage door
invariably the fawning women are engrossed by his candlestick
it's well-established that Alyo Kazaz favors beaches in a big way
the saint hollers incantations as he delouses the wise men
"indeed, how much longer?" says the primeval snake to the reproachful doctor

Ivan regularly pleads that his roof is on fire
the mathematician promenades in a gulley with Danitsa
alarmed townspeople swarm with pots & pans
Nikola addresses his food: "you are not what matters"
gravediggers sing the praises of motorcycles for business reasons

[SHORE 5: VIENNA]

Gerhart on the Alps: "although far-reaching, not insurmountable"
in the absence of other plans, Irlen pants for breath profoundly in Vienna
opera singers in red stiffly duel
& an exemplary deserter lectures schoolboys on the inferiority complex
Gustav, choking in the sanatorium: "I am experiencing a
           metamorphosis!"
at daybreak sleepwalking torsos make slimy, guttural noises
a tribunal of girls will hear remarks from an insignificant little man
wretched substitute for Otto the butcher, who has gone ice-skating
the unchaste psychoanalyst sneezes about his inexplicable sexual
           problem

the bothersome devil has no decency & has given Aunt Victorine free rein
the naked governess, who has weak intestines, pokes shyly at a pair of
           trousers
her name, horribly, is Isadora; the whole neighborhood
without an image to feed on or serious thoughts of marriage
tells neurotic fairy tales about her to the undertaker

Nina the cabaret dancer to the fortune-teller: "everything you say is laughable"
a faint knock on the door; have a look at the prostitutes' wares
"I cannot account for this oppression" says Bruno sitting at the piano
"what happened today was evil; I've always kept it to myself"
Giuseppe the seducer has bad news for your country home

[SHORE 6: NOWADAYS IN AFRICA]

nowadays in Africa two or three dollars is enough for a duffel bag
we leave what had been a garden at dusk & step into a miserably small boat
people have been needing toothbrushes & are full of dung
whipping out her beliefs Zabeth is willing to pay for it
ANNOUNCING: A SMALL NUMBER OF CROCODILES SIXTY MILES
              AWAY
indistinguishable in the hubbub of wanderers wailing "fuck you!"
at a couple on the outskirts of lovemaking
Gujarat, frothing, wiping his lips: "where did you get this?"
chanting about the Koran & its laws beneath all that remains of a
              monument

in the colonial style Ferdinand is going into the desert with his little plastic
              bags
the sorceress has no boundaries: "the house isn't on fire, is it?"
frontiersmen topple folk sayings, which is cause for offense to many
the rainy season is responsible for the skeleton of the merchant sailor
& the sturdy Belgian doesn't want his dogs chained

even the dumb scientists know about Mahesh's fetish
Iyanda: "what does this spurt of blood mean?"
the physicist is pretending to be a shadow on honeymoon
a little time in the weeds with Polly goes a long way
Salim goes off to play hide-&-seek with some freeloaders

[SHORE 7: THE ABBOT]

a well-meaning adult, Yu Jang marches through the fields with a sword
the prince bumps into an ill-bred monk at a bend in the river
holding teapots the villagers display their teeth to the ambassador
moreover, the abbot is reviewing the death list in the temple courtyard
Yeesun fires a .357 revolver at the stucco walls
the difference is that it's dawn & the plaintiff is cutting the elephant grass
two undertakers leave the dais; "let's go catch some rats"
Janthorn's parrot is indifferent
streets are deserted; the boxer has gone to referee the husbanding

Phraidam: "however high heaven may arch above us,
"like the cobra or the phoenix we must endure the bitter with the sweet"
on a winding path Abbot Nian gives a candidate for pastry chef a fond,
   gentle squeeze
some men speak as if music & mashed beans should console us;
you can wave your hand all you want at precious stones

Feng the usurper has a nightmare about scarecrows & assumes the lotus position
for lack of a buffalo Mrs. Han shouts "woe betide you!" at the vermillion war
   horse
the general to his chariot: "is it nirvana you're after?
"what's wrong with you?!"—Wu Yang has been led astray by error
apparently his concubines have erected an altar to pythons

[SHORE 8: ST. PETERSBURG]

the starchy landlady isn't concerned about the shooting sparks
still chewing, the locksmith is straightforward with his religion of girls
"oh, you are awful!"—two or three people with diamond rings to Katerina
we're expecting about eighty government officials, I wouldn't mess with it
the monkey gargles cold water at the card players
"surely it isn't my punishment coming upon me?" says Sonia as we tie a fat noose
          on her
"that's enough, now" says the deceitful madman in his ecstasy
loathsome Amalia comes in from the veranda with an indignant rustle of
          silk
"she has excellent qualities" she says triumphantly as she forks over the six rubles

greedy Zossimov has revolution beef
with Darya's friend the freshly-laundered painter
"everybody looks down on us" says the rent-collector to his glass of milk
Marmeladov wrings his hands disparagingly as he enjoys his morals
the fact is, the prostitute was very young, very pretty

& she has absentmindedly tainted my lawyer in this time of loss
what's more, blood-stained Raskolnikov is making his selection
St. Petersburg blows a kiss at the victim of psychology
Lizaveta like a panic-stricken owl: "it's all that cuckoo's fault!!"
& other such behavior, as good manners require

[SHORE 9: THE YALTA ZOO]

"it's enough to make one cry" says the ostrich Olenka has been teasing
say goodbye to the lion; the will of God has no sense of humor
Sashenka is taking a lesson in guile from a hyena
which one spider calls "an absurd & evil activity!"
are meat pies poison to elephants, do you know?
"what a queer fellow you are!" says Ariadne to a stinky jackal
though a daughter of commoners, no lack of boldness
one of Lubkov's henchmen makes a pass at her young & lovely body
but they're apples & oranges, & besides, I've beaten him to it

ignoring the bald gentleman, Ariadne leans her cleavage into the giraffe
        enclosure
it was Nikola's idea to visit the Yalta zoo; we practically had a war over it
I was a little vexed but I'm having a nice time
the colonel has worldly motives, says those two rogues don't jingle
        properly
Polinka when we get back to her drawing-room: "hoorah! alas!"

when no one is looking Ariadne struggles desperately out of her lace
& I smash a crystal decanter in the process of devouring her
after sex we do some lamplight nudes
out the window church spires on white sky
we'd better get back in there

[SHORE 10: THE GALA]

"I won't make a secret of it" Samoylenko begins
like a blind man describing luxury
"how true it is!" lies Horikawa at the banquet table
quite unlike spinach, I think to myself,
gazing out the window at the paintbrush pine-trees
cheerless, unprofitable mushrooms come next
yawn.... a picnic in the middle of an earthquake would be preferable
everybody's wearing masks but me
I should have read the damn invitation

Yuziki, lifting up her skirt in an obscene curtsy: "define 'silent,' your excellency"
five minutes later her costume is crumpled in a corner of the emperor's
            bedroom
contorted like a cat over the monarch the heroine embraces non-
            resistance to evil
"nonsense" he says as she climbs frantically back into her petticoat
almost forgetting to untie the ropes that bind our fearless leader to his
            bedposts

as usual the samurai have been given free rein to throw forks at each other
no trouble at all for the malodorous nobles but I sit next to them
meanwhile, Osumi has defiantly fallen in love with a gardener (absurd)
your mama's potatoes, we all agree, are extraordinary

[SHORE 11: THE VILLAIN]

turns out culprit Alexey has been ushering ladies of higher rank into coffins
"why weep?" says Fyodor sagely
the undertaker has not entirely forgotten the heiress's sing-song voice
obediently doing what must be done to dried-up Adelaida
shadowy ladies chuckle out their theories on the villain "of breeding & delicacy"
mahogany Nikita says there are three types of wretches:
obstinate, thrashing, & deserving of sympathy
"I detest this violent business" says devil's advocate Dmitri
the meal is by no means grim; I am a hair's breadth from the girl they call crazy

the counterfeit slut is sent off to waken Pavel
"let me think" says the doctor
"allow me to ask: was Grushenka even capable of health?"
with friends like these there's no need for a summer house
although I'd take the gallows over pleasantries any day

Ariadne starts a game of under-the-table footsie
"what's the matter with loss of life?" she says fixing her bonnet
in the aristocratic semi-darkness you can't see the rivets in Nancy
who is apparently "so done with this rigmarole about murder"
"but where is the proof?" says Dmitri, dragging it up again...

[SHORE 12: HIROSHIMA]

in unfortunate Hiroshima the enemy's bomb got Shigematsu
"FORGET SELF! ALL OUT FOR YOUR COUNTRY"—the writing on the wall
air raid sirens turn banker faces green
Yasuko, pleasantly, is not among the scorched
a nervous & fearful factory owner: "come now, woman"
the flames thwart Matsumoto even, drawing-room & all
by midday the doctors run out of white crosses
running away three gentlemen's mantra: *mens sana in corpore sano*
"where are you going, sonny?" says the mushroom cloud to the aristocrats

bleeding refugees carrying clocks & fish baskets
rationed rice smothered in chemicals
Shokichi saw all sorts of things from the holes where his windows were
mangled bodies mixed in brick heaps
the city still smolders

trapped in smoke, stabbing pains, & sobs
forbidden ideas RE: the men who did this
"quite impossible, I'm afraid" says dead president
imagine it: Harry Truman naked & alone in that burning wasteland
above a pile of naked corpses, written in charcoal: *mens sana in corpore*
     sano

[SHORE 13: THE HIGH TIDE HOTEL]

lathered in saltwater haul ourselves up the beach to the High Tide Hotel
Barcenas looking rather stately until he spills coffee on the pool table
"I am the destructive type" he says fumbling forty francs
Dmitri, walking in with a fishing pole from the jetty: "I see a little hope"
which is super false; our procession of damp thighs take up café tables 11-
        15
"you will never be a saint" says Nikola the rent-collector to his unbuttered
        roll
neckbeard Poplerin lifts up his shirt to reveal a ridiculous chest tattoo
"surprise!"—it says *introibo ad altare Dei*—"feel how smooth!"
I slide Ariadne my room key

she squeals as I slobber in the tuft of hair between her legs
"I'm trying to be a good girl" holding her untied bikini top over her breasts
meanwhile in the café, her cuck husband Gerhart: "explain that!"
wicked Komiya: "let's go get some opium!"
"twelve quid" says Ferdinand in the quarter of town where 600% profits are made

"God be praised!" says Domingo piously smoking
"nothing like drugs to cheer up a fellow whose roof is on fire" says Ivan
"shut your eyes, then!" says the devil to noisy Gujarat
Darya's friend Alyo Kazaz, the painter: "look! it's Grushenka's ghost!"
"your hat is a little crushed" says Ariadne as we noticeably return to the party

[SHORE 14: A HAPPY CHRISTMAS]

at the 8-course dinner my lawyer takes up the duty of smiling
"what a coward you are!" says flared-up Seliphan to reactionary Zossimov
Ariadne's boyish blue eyes catch me staring at the gold locket between her
        breasts
"oh, good heavens" says the doctor as Takichiro brandishes a scythe
he's a great deal drunk & an active member of the Communist Party
I slip out with Ariadne & get lost in the labyrinth lit by tiny red lamps
"we might as well" she says as we violently conquer an empty room
10 minutes later we're perspiring naked under the out-of-place
        chandelier

"I'll be frank; you're a doll but this has to stop"
trying to ward off caution I ask "what would satisfy you?
"of course, it's a good idea, but..."—I hear laughter from downstairs
"we're missing the soup" she says with a soft smile
I utter a multitude of protests: "but what for? what necessary steps?"
we climb somewhat tearful out of bed & grope for our underwear

in the drawing room the birds are putting two & two together;
        everybody's smoking
"it is our fate" Ariadne whispers to me; O how askew the scales of justice!
Giuseppe is ranting about the government & "the nature of things:
not from knowledge but from three glasses of vodka
"happy Christmas Grigori" says Gerhart, offering a gift basket; all are in good
        spirits

[SHORE 15: PARIS]

"to be sure!" says disheveled Horikawa, sniffing the stone slabs of corpulent Paris
with a failed wink the well-groomed diplomat escorts Yuziki to the bank of the
        Seine
urgent passerby chant "whose progress? no one's progress!"
Takichiro springs up to join them like a moth to a flame
at a café shaded by chestnut trees we discuss the big issues & the stench of urine
the backstabbing Belgian: "the capitalist class is hardly superfluous"
"it's impossible to respect you, my dear fellow" says Fyodor vomiting
bashful Nikola has an oppressive conscience & clears his throat
"I am rarely busy" he says throwing up his hands

bearing false witness ad infinitum sumptuous Sonia has no grasp of reality
hoodwinked Ruzhdi has bitterly opted for the quiet life
Nozdrev laughs at Polinka's slavishly fashionable petticoat
I blow my nose at him; "the grownups have to talk"
"I read that dusk is a symbol of masculinity" says Mr. Sada

crab-eyed Raskolnikov is ogling Ariadne; worthless Pedro stumbles into a taxi
we leave the café for the subdued light of a cabaret
whipping out cigarettes as we take our seats
hurriedly philosophizing Poplerin orders a big piece of cheese
& in the spirit of the age Ariadne says to me "may I sit down & dream with
        you?"

KAREN

1

In white slacks a playful fella dined in prewar splendor. Where is Queen Victoria? The messenger in a burst of generosity scrambled in zigzags across the wedding. Within days the time came for a lady of the highest rank to straight away emigrate to the film capital. The only issue to be addressed is that of the babies on top of piles of furniture. In the parlor of Coco Chanel the heathen explained that he was going away for a while. To let him return to Aubazine in a matter of days after his coming ashore can only be described as ridiculous. The widow without regaining consciousness sucked on a pipe. Those people weren't sick in their heads!—very well. The streets of Paris were the scene of perilous moments & Stravinsky. This is Karen.

2

Became even harder the times. Karen was asking a nation that had given up its Wednesday to think of a weak army from a feudal society. Just as the trees outside the window were not plants but little speeches, the decision to drop Nixon from the ticket had fallen in on itself. Soon her friends began to worry about the wraparound veranda; whatever authority was in charge always made Karen feel as if the secrets were nothing so mundane as the largest employer in the country. She said that she knew we would all do our best to leave behind the Republican National Committee. Her voice was high & nervous; even Bill had his rain hat on. Long ago, when a little freedom was more important than security, Karen hurried across the mown grass.

3

Hazy weather intervened that spring; the established opinion is that Karen ate raisins as early as sixteen. There was, of course, a desire to avoid falling into the hands of cannibals; on the other side of the island, rightly or wrongly, Bill had plunged himself into his remarkable verbal facility. With patience & labor, Karen, in her innocence, was inclined to exaggerate the waves. In addition to looking back on her past life with horror, she could not yet scrape together a companion. Although there was no immediate financial pressure, at about eight yards' distance Bill constituted a mast & sail for the boat that was her life. It was a truth, however, that Bill was a bad carpenter. A disappointment, chiefly. The wreck of the good life bestowed on Karen legitimate afflictions.

4

After two weeks on the tree-lined road to infinity Karen couldn't help feeling the injustice of the parable of the sower. People began calling her Manna; Bill honked his horn gently. With alcohol & cotton swabs Karen universalized her blood. Then, in late July, Bill pulled up alongside to oppose the idea. A banquet was held in Paris to celebrate a flattened pack of cigarettes & with a dash of lavender the finest carpenter (an estranged son of the middle class) nursed a child. To convey the brute sexuality she saw in Bill, Karen applied thick strokes of unruly youngsters to the canvas.

5

At the designated time, his words hurried, Bill described the long sweet nightmare of his marriage to Lila. His story shows that a bulging brown paper bag full of stock certificates secured with a rubber band is invariably legitimate. The road to San Antonio was straightforward & nobody cared what happened to his dark good looks. The car, despite a misunderstanding or two, pulled up at the motel throughout the year. Lila was psychotic, dangerously so; to make up for lost time Karen & Bill chuckled gently in the dark, their tones taut & breaking, the blinds drawn. Wouldn't it be wonderful if they were still doing well today?

6

You could replace the money & no one would ever know. Though modest in size, Bill entered the small, enclosed backyard. As cotton workers assumed an important role in leaning against the bureau smoking, the first wave of mechanized cotton spinning came to continental Europe as a direct result of the table being set for Bill in the kitchen. The soil & climate of the Caribbean was well-suited to holding the dish & chewing. Without access to capital, Bill rose & stood over Karen with his hand on her bowed head. Physical proximity was one way to establish the darkness; by the late nineteenth century Bill was locking the front door. To flourish, he required knowledge of the trivial matters of her day. It certainly helped him produce a small china effigy of a rooster. When the guns fell silent, he lit a cigarette; any hint of demise was hiding in a clump of shrubbery.

7

In any event, there they were, like two different species, burping out a few false words demurely. At three o'clock, in accordance with the almost universal belief in the Antichrist, Bill began to get annoyed by the clock. It may seem fanciful, but I suspect the walls were painted to look like rock barnacles. Karen was a nurse; Bill, a geologist. Both hovered achingly close to conversational sterility. Psychologically, they were vegetables: no laughing baby, no meaningful dialogue, no resisting of destruction by our native animals. Ils ont cherché une chenille.

8

It will be part of our object in this chapter to see his face. Every individual at his birth is flung into the grass, & Bill was no different. There is a sense in which I believe most firmly that Bill was the last person in the world to want to deal with the bedroom. What, then, was Karen doing? As a rule, she was a monster—but she was *his* monster. It is important to notice that most women think of nothing but the tendency of all governments to deteriorate. If Bill suffered, which can only be denied by stretching one's hand out over an open fire, it must be borne in mind that he deserved it. What was the use of him making & entering into an association for the purpose of satisfying a common want? A mere similarity or coincidence of object, while it may lead for a time to very close cooperation in pursuit of that object, does not necessarily imply that the ashes would never blow toward them with the salt wind from the sea.

9

It is essential to the existence of the schoolmaster for us to consider once more whether or not it is really better to dance alone. When Jesus preached his sermon on the mount, why did the schoolmaster bite his nails? It would seem as if there were clothes thrown all over the place. The same thing happened in the kitchen. To the extent to which the schoolmaster is restrained from accumulating marriages, men who may well have been no more gifted than the he blinked, looking at the blue sky through the open window. The unity of civilized life depends on people saying "that woman" when they dislike a person, & the schoolmaster very much disliked Karen. The development of the machine stands in no simple relation to the development of a dinner hastily swallowed.

10

One explanation for Bill's silence on the subject of Yugoslavia was that he loved it like an old friend. From the speed at which the convoy traveled, Bill supposed that art is a harmony parallel to nature. Children gathered around storytellers who gave them impassioned accounts of the human form. Bill sighed. According to sages of every stripe he was merely an apologist for the establishment. Bill's mom knew all about our whole society being ashamed of him. At the time of his triumphant concert in 1895, Marseille was covered in snow. Now, even Karen won't take his calls. It just goes to show that when the mask is pulled off, men are known for what they actually are, & their coal-black reputation is dragged through the streets. As one philosopher put it, "His mouth fell open, & his tongue protruded, & he looked hideous." Anguished, helpless, Bill went to the head of the stairs yelling for Karen. I can think of no higher praise.

11

Because of the war, vultures flapped at the edge of the clearing. Let the truth be seen! Karen built a fire in the iron stove. At 2 AM, sunburned wildly dressed people began to launch unprecedented rescues. It was very bad. Throughout the great deluge Karen chain-smoked Shermans in a parking lot. Helicopters flew overhead. Then it was time for a poker- playing, gregarious entertainment wizard to make a tasteless joke about death. Through a demanding combination of hourly prayer & harmless gossip, Karen got the news out. She is the most beautiful woman I have ever seen.

12

It's embarrassing as fuck. Bill ran up to try & comfort her but even with binoculars the villagers couldn't make out the French. Bill adopted a wait-&-see attitude; Karen purchased a souvenir ashtray. Six days after that, Bill sprained his ankle getting off a commercial airliner in San Diego. Turns out he's not an electrical engineer after all. What were these follies? Past the three-blocks-long scale model of America a Secret Service-type guy initiated a card game. Partly out of guilt Karen clawed her way back to Winnipeg, where Bill had passed the point of no return. His distrust extended to a fleet of fishing boats. Shortly before four in the morning the weather changed & Bill wondered if humidity could shrink your jeans. If it could, he could be in trouble. No moving picture director could have planned a better entrance for Reggie.

13

As I have now spoken of blinded Bill & coincidence Karen, it is time to speak of Reggie. Numberless instances might be given of his unthinkingly holding my hands under the hot water tap to thaw them; it is the nature of men to be as much bound by farm boy Bill as by middle-aged widow Karen. Some may wonder how it came about that Bill disappeared down the pleasant path to evil, & the answer is Reggie. Reggie's wickedness was accompanied by such a vigor of mind & body that he once stole a district attorney's Plymouth. I will not here speak of Karen's desire to run as fast & far away as possible. I conclude by saying that this new bed-partner of mine is a good judge of character.

14

Here was a typical case of ringworm, there a case of Bill getting up slowly & walking over to the cabinet in the corner of his office. Bullets began to sing over my head & I became increasingly impatient to return home. For two days & nights Karen held out her arms in a deprecatory gesture; under the circumstances it would be disastrous to cross a small river. Smoke from several fires was plainly visible. Falling into a state of listlessness, Karen brought forth a ponderous remark about the war situation. There was really no danger. Without exception she wore a long wine-colored smock. By the same token, Reggie went snooping into the business of private citizens. As a mark of courtesy Bill nodded his head slowly as he sat, unnoticed, alone, in the cabin of the airliner flying over fields & woods & rivers.

15

In 1615 the weather became too inclement for outdoor assemblies. In Augsburg & Memmingen, & perhaps in other cities as well, Karen had spoken the truth: "Box them up. Keep them in a dry place where they will suffer no further decay." Orphans & other poor children, ready to make friends but not over-eager to the point of condescension, took up linen spinning. Having brought no camping equipment other except a pair of camel's-hair rugs, Bill received only a modest salary. There had been almost no conversation between them as they trudged along the well-beaten highway to Strasburg. In every medieval city the sun shone & the sky was blue.

ADDICTION

The balloon has been popped & the man who was holding it has been arrested because he was not the same man who bought it; rather he was a different man, a very bad man named Jonathan who upon release from jail immediately went & stole yet another balloon. The road to becoming a serial balloon thief was not long. Step one: desire balloon. Step two: no money. Step three: steal balloon. Jonathan was practically addicted to balloons. He just had to have them at any cost. Balloons made him feel safe & youthful, two things which, due to his age (42) and nemesis (Dr. Causebad), he was not. There had, admittedly, once been a time when he was both safe & youthful, but that time was passed. It had been more than twenty years since he had been young & free from the evil works of Dr. Causebad. His relationship with Dr. Causebad was inextricably linked with his balloon addiction. He was a mere sixteen years old when he purchased his first balloon. It was a red balloon. Lately he has become interested in balloons with special messages written on them like, 'Congratulations!" & "Sorry   for your   loss!"   &   "Happy   Fiftieth Anniversary!" Really any kind of balloon will do, though. He just needs his fix, & he needs it three & sometimes four times a day. Dr. Causebad is not supportive of Jonathan's enthusiasm for balloons, in fact he opposes it. He even prescribes medication to mitigate the cravings, but addiction is such a cunning enemy of life that Jonathan has long since lost the power to do anything about it. He used to buy a balloon once a week but now he needs at least three a day which is why he steals them. Sometimes he gets caught but usually he doesn't because the people he steals them from are usually either very small or busy celebrating their anniversary or what have you. By the time they notice the missing balloon, Jonathan is long gone.

THE LOBBY

Something will have to be done about the lobby.
There's rainwater pouring in from the ceiling in the lobby.
There are far too many people in the lobby.
There's a noisy breakup taking place in the lobby.
I can't even hear myself think in the lobby.
There are two events competing for attention in the lobby.
A child has been abandoned in the lobby.
A man with two heads has entered the lobby.
A woman who says her name is Carla was just addressed as Josephine in the lobby.
Don't you think four hundred & sixty people is too many people in the lobby?
Have you no decency? Have you no sense? Was I hired to just watch as chaos unfurls
       its red banner in the lobby?
A fight has broken out in the lobby.
Someone's quoting Karl Marx in the lobby.
The employees are unionizing in the lobby.
Management is nowhere to be found in the lobby.
Someone's asking to speak with a manager & I don't know what to tell them. It's really
       getting out of hand in the lobby.
Somebody brought their pet giraffe into the lobby.
This is ridiculous. I can only take so much more of this lobby.
A man is selling discount staplers in the lobby.
I don't think that's appropriate at all.
Another man is scalping hockey tickets in the lobby.
What a joke. An impromptu rock concert has begun in the lobby.
A mass is being held in the lobby.
A baby has been born in the lobby.
An old woman named Lucy has died in the lobby.
Her husband is talking about damages in the lobby.
The media have showed up to see what all the fuss is about in the lobby.
The ghost of Ezra Pound has been caged in the lobby.
How do you even do that? I'm getting fed up with this lobby.
I've had it up to here with this lobby.
We've run out of luggage carts in the lobby.
A soccer team just arrived in the lobby.

Two couples are fighting over the bridal suite in the lobby.

The police have been called in the lobby.

There's barely room to wave your arms & shout "ladies & gentleman!" in the lobby.

Under other circumstances I would enjoy the rock concert that's taking place in the lobby.

The baby has been named Lucy after the woman who died in the lobby.

The giraffe has gotten its head stuck in the ceiling in the lobby.

The carpet is soaked with rainwater in the lobby.

The priest has just consecrated the holy host in the lobby.

The soccer team has started a scrimmage in the lobby.

The couple who broke up have gotten back together in the lobby.

The person quoting Karl Marx has changed his mind & is now a capitalist in the lobby.

The two events which once competed for attention have merged to form one big event in the lobby.

The abandoned child has been adopted in the lobby.

The man with two heads has had a nose job in the lobby.

The confusion with regard to the woman allegedly named Carla but actually named Josephine has been cleared up in the lobby.

It was all just a big misunderstanding. The fight has turned into an orgie in the lobby.

The employees' union has been brutally crushed in the lobby.

Management has arrived in the lobby.

The man who was selling discount staplers has run out of staplers & is now whoring out his body to travelling businessmen in the lobby.

The man selling hockey tickets is now preaching the gospel of Jesus Christ our Lord & savior in the lobby.

The priest is handing out holy communion in the lobby.

The police have arrived in the lobby.

The police have opened fire in the lobby.

Something will have to be done about the lobby.

DAY'S WORK

The day has done its work on me
& water floating fixed; starless & late
I cough out forgettable certainties,
in the using up of drinks sprawl out.
It cannot be now the same red that it was
or the sun so useful scorching—
take this with you, through the narrows,
through the roads curving they catch us loosely grasping,
on one side the ditch of shadows, innocuous,
& of course that same old girl.
When the alignment of chemicals
sheds life on what has only been used before for drowning
take this buoyant memory, cards closing,
take it where it will provide what otherwise would not be there.

A RENDERING

chrome fittings cast me on gray floors
or throw me out evenhandedly at random
with no regard for towers.
escaped who knows me
won't. run from the men of shiny locks,
hair shaven & muscles atrophied with amnesiac splay
grip some leaning white picket fence flowered
as Hot Dog stands in the veil of Manhattan.
Chrome fittings question me at great length & loudly
Or forget the whole deed completely
In a sycophantic nod to a conceptualization of Neighborliness.
Dumped on some highway stumble blindly toward a pancake
And Brain Squeezed Up In Confused Lemonade Ventures
so Far from the liberties hocked for veil manhattan

HER COLORS

Tigering woods with siren lights they will dog me, closing
in desert motel pools it will be necessary to dive down,
farther than I could in the cul-de-sac of her colors.
Blinds peeking ash tip & boxers pace the room,

map out state highways & leave late,
as late as I wanted to in the cul-de-sac of her colors.
White line it west or wherever, skirt cops & hat on,
dawn's gray naked

more than I ever was in the cul-de-sac of her colors.
Some diner: order as random as the elements of my disguise,
give me please the recommended amount
as nourishing as her colors

. Then I will check the charge,
& surrender the table: scraps of cotton, her colors lint.

EX-GIRLFRIENDS & THE WATER CYCLE

Dew papers my head inform in from outside's August
to slurp it black before clocking in that office geometry
whose boss will bigtime vulturing see over
me screen the hours box.
Surge turnstiles & platforms damming us, bottled, belted
we spill from gutters & break hearts on wine's opacity.
Paid we stutter see-yous & idly sidewalks rush down, drops
on windshield. We ended up
on the floor & since it was the weekend we went to the park
during which our sense of self-worth evaporated.
I watched a bead of sweat traverse a tit
& you saw some guy's junk as he jogged.
Dew trash, clothes; rivulets of condescensions
which I ought to have washed off by now.

THE DELIVERY DRIVER

Succulent. Aisles in library lights this number
repeats title hyperbole: Never Cries
but her eyes accuse me birdfast with a swish of black bangs.
Never cries, never cries, never mistake a parking lot for a helipad.
Evil bitch, or said so. Aisles' vanishing point, her
leaving like a light off at the end of the hall
& the next time
I saw her

        sunred sun its anointing of the windows of cars
        apparently a pull for us..
        elected a second-chance hour, delivered her door as if a body
        of tides rose water necessarily
        for the skinny price of eight bucks to the moon.

THE PROCESS PRIEST (A THEME)

Pod chrysalitics & to seed stone wallings off
For the fusing forces that the drivers in hand
Plaid cropcream dadbod on the fairways
Make a few calls to.

Phasing & fad we buy into the pyramid schema, such that
no one walks.
Worship with us, mushroom cloud;
Bodies burned & bodies bowed.

Somebody told me once that once where
nobody knew numbers like zero or sixty billion
a village proceeded all in black
to carry coffins.
I know it's true
because I'm taking this history class & it seems to be a theme.

THE MARCH OF THE MOURNING

Sceptered exceptions to the MasterCard crumbs
are we, we whispering "what?" we (1)
don't believe in your December we
(2) will however explain hold
her hand—your hand—hold me—I want to cry—

(3) Just because you a thing
just because orange Mussolini
just because "just because," & Other Bad Preludes
we were infinite cliché
really did I love you

Really did the moon make losers of our light
Really did the night make morning
                              mourn the way
                              only it can.

TO A READER

Translated from the French of Charles Baudelaire

Mistakes & stupidness, sins & greed
work our bodies, fill up our heads,
even our amiable guilt is fed
like the bums who tend to their parasites' needs.

Our repentance is loose & our sins hold tight—
we pay so much to let off the load
returning happy to the muddy road
as if dirty tears could clean what once was white.

Satan, that motherfucker, was at our bed
dazzling us with his horseshit,
& his alchemy boiled every bit
of our volition—vapor. Off it sped.

The devil is our puppeteer!
Smelly trinkets charm us
& the daily descending does not alarm us—
nose-deaf to the darkness in which we disappear.

Like the wretches who F. & suck
the tits of an old whore
we secretly glance through an open door,
chew a shriveled orange which we plucked

from the hiving demons like maggots infesting
our trashed brain.
Into our lungs death drains,
an unseen sewer, to our choked protesting.

If rape & drugs & daggers & fire
have not embroidered their nice little designs
on the banal canvas of our destiny with dotted lines
it's because our souls are tired

from dancing in this den of jackals & lice,
apes & vultures & scorpions & snakes.
The cacophony of their howling shakes
this menagerie of known vices

which holds something more ugly, more unclean—
a growth. It does not wave its arms or yell
but under its supervision the world fell
apart; it has swallowed us with a yawn. Very unclean.

Apathy! Reluctantly it cries
in a back booth of a hookah bar
& you know it, because you are
my brother, with your two-faced lies.

GOLDEN VERSES

Translated from the French of Gerard de Nerval

"Eh, what! everything is sentient!"
-Pythagoras

Free-thinker man: do you suppose yourself sole
in this world, Life bursting around you now?
Freedom the forces you hold in allow
but in your councils the universe has no role.

Respect in the beast a moving mind;
to Nature a soul per flower's born
& metals the mystery of Love adorn.
"Everything senses..." & powers all about you bind.

Fear the sparing blind wall's gaze:
to matter are verbs attached as well;
do not make them serve your impious ways.

Often in creatures obscure gods dwell,
under the lids of little eyes still closed,
& under the surface of stones, pure spirit grows...

DELFICA

Translated from the French of Gerard de Nerval

"Ultima Cumaei venit jam carminis aetas."

Do you know it, Daphne? That ancient romance
under sycamore & olive trees, under laurels' white
blooms, myrtle & willow, trembling & flight?
The repeating love song's familiar dance?

Do you remember the pillars of the Temple's façade,
& the bitter lemons you sunk your teeth in?
The cave, deadly to visiting fools, wherein
the vanquished dragon sleeps with its seed? These gods

for whom you're always weeping
will be back! Time will bring back the order of days gone by;
the earth has shuddered with a prophetic sigh.

Still the Latin-faced sibyl is sleeping
under the Arch of Constantine
—& nothing has disturbed the severe portico.

TWO PUNKS

across the street
punk on
stoop smoke swallows airplane
I can hear his partner shrug off ties
while I'm waiting like the business card on their windowsill
which offers something exclusive in a narrow sans serif
no one said the safe word so why did you stop?

out in space
a broken satellite
transmits a final zero
whatever that means
& the punks kiss in the rain

ALWAYS FOR THE FIRST TIME

but I heard different, that stump of knife hearts the
hand so sword loves a wall in a museum
we met at a museum but we don't meet there
there were yardsticks a mile long
& long paintings made by computers & a stern woman told
me not to touch a portrait which clearly

                said
"The room in which I was made is now
open sky through which glide without incident those
birds survivor, helicopters, & since
        I was made in the future folks
code thryou on jetpacks & like
—O fuming dissipation of exhaust machines' black fumes! it
made it made it *made*, O it made laurels in the sky!"

it said I could not possibly understand & autonot try—
the wreck of a coal train to a dog
lifting leg on graffiti boxcar . . .

                              do you remember the
woods
a clearing where yellow sun fell on a log
a clearing where   yellow sun fell on a log

beavers had eaten aspen line the path
yes I remembered, & after we talked at the museum we
had sex at her place & after that
she made tea, what kind of tea do you want?

ST. LOUIS DOM

    I tell her I want my own helicopter
       normally   I pretend otherwise
but she's a self-serving narcissist as well

she stares at the fridge
like she's a seashell that somehow ended up in a lake

her curving-to-the-carpet spine as
  she ties her shoes
   before throwing a shirt on— the
  television is talking up war
but how should I know shoelace intentions

there is a great urgency to the curtain's opening up like
   the rush of air on a subway platform
        hairpins before
        a dance

against the background of chain link moiré

THE QUEEN OF DIAMONDS

diamonds you buy a ticket
to see anything else fold forks
ribbons & wires are worthless in small pieces

it's what she looks at right after she looks at you

table four is a comprehensive guide written in
black lipstick

THE MORNING AFTER

drunk plaids jaywalk to the point of neon
whose viaduct we hop as giggle our skin
gone by the breaking news of liquid relationship
puddle up clothes or scaffold over silver
she's on the other side of the room so am I
worn flat black & shiny, the other kicked off shoe

last dawn I saw the sun
her building flowers
in line with previous
still
rather
like fist out of the passenger side window
evenings which walking back turn heads

THE GAMBLER

for Joseph Suh

"how are you supposed to meet girls?" he said sitting
            at his desk
which I considered clean to the point of unhealthy my
reply was sarcastic, in retrospect even cruel
            someday I'll come back & tell you
                        what I said ///
up down is this what you want she asked
Joseph didn't like me bringing girls over
            but I did when he was gone

he was so Catholic he
thought I was possessed by the devil
because I talk in my sleep
I had to tell a university administrator
that my proud red poems were not Satanist in nature
Joe punched a hole in the wall
when he found out I had sex on his bed
"safe sex matters, Joe, top bunks are dangerous," I said

this kid and me, we hated each other

he used to keep a statue of Mary on his desk &
on the midnight road back from Chicago
I saw people throwing themselves out
in front of me . . . not the stairs the architects the
stairs I'm talking about
a math major addicted to scratchers

                        * * *

in case of fire
do not
use elevator
laugh with someone sad, while you are
                                    walking

PUT DOWN

I put it down on top of the flowers
forgot the example of an impersonal mountain
heavy dark winter spruce wind
of cold external factors preceded by a
pile of sticks & leaves
dictating the establishment sphere

I put it down on top of the flowers
forgot the examples of timid moons
daylight masks on blank blue shivers before snow of
catcalling shadows animal as
the air gets thinner
penetrating approximate but benevolent irregularities

I put it down on top of the flowers
I couldn't remember the story about the marvelous orchard casual
fountain by the beautiful girls
who have less liberty to congeal on their corneas
than the men who hang out of the windows of corner offices

positing a racket, some sort of patriarchal design,
I dropped it on purpose to smash the (comparison to) flowers

LADIES AND GENTLEMEN, THE CIRCUS

she wears a
circus marquee
for a dress
& I love her for it

her mother brings us a bowl of cherries on the front porch
in the telephone pole pink dusk
gosh

I went to the Pruitt-Igoe site once in the middle of the night

sometimes I think language is a straitjacket
other times, like right now,
as I sit in the Del Taco Starbucks overhearing
I think language is more like a sauna—
the degree to which it is refreshing
is negatively correlated with the number of people who
shit I can't say that everybody does that

I wanted to use
the word "threadbare"
but, not having found a place for it, I don't think I will

this whole thing is just for show
you start to think

THE MARCH OF THE RIOT POLICE

somewhere in the city mythic PULL
up to it while the altar shot's on me
cigarette smoke fuzz face in red mirror
cop sirens are the dorsal fins of the American city
it was like angels & demons when I heard it on the radio until
the march of the riot police

LIVE from Ferguson after the weather report
a cumulonimbus formation on W. Florissant now
folks we are expecting clouds of tear gas
time for a little commercial break but stay tuned for
The March of the Riot Police™

NOT WHAT WE IMAGINED IN THE WAITING ROOM

With final line from a Tristan Tzara poem

CHICAGO: glows a ballooning hospital where check
is ready whenever you are not sure
which way on sixty-second
weaving the urban swaddle of Pantone yuppies
whose financial advisors spotted a real opportunity here with these
crumby tablets, cross magazines, you're not you when your hungry
GMO'd voters in training line up for potty breaks
Jolly Ranchers recess bell curve life expecting
there is a reason for the phrase;
maternity ward mortality in America
you can go years without ever hearing

a friendly HAND OVER LOCAL DEEDS
the corporation made glass opaque it can do the same to your eyes

glows a law professor whose former student
wanted him to see her baby daughter,
who with big eyes articulate big disappointment
wit de world & its odd pockets
what a wonder a child's brain can be
Mom got shot by police the following Thursday
because twenty-oh-four thought twenty-oh-five
might be harboring a Bin Laden
on the plus side the next twenty years
are gonna be one big daddy daughter dance at twenty-oh-six

oh-h-h say can you SEEEEEE/ the jolly roger?

whatever we imagined in the waiting room
Wrigley applause can be heard from
the alley next door
crenellated right up to the apex of god"

IT RAINS ON THE TOWN

sea wall
the puddle you do not have permission to enter
repeat: swipe, through the turnstile you go,
engaging in conversation with the least likely
old man who was kind enough to give me a stack of subway passes
when I ran out of money in Paris

a splash cannot be heard from great distance

but likening a splash to a kiss
might last,
or maybe the sea dries up, just up & evaporates,
but this has been thought of: it rains
very hard
on the town

how often have I
when the rain was loud on the roof
thought of Webster how
—how often shivering thought of nothing at all

say to the sea wall: do you not wonder
who it is out there, & how they're faring

in the storm
she slammed the door
I sat there with great anxiety
I can feel it even from great distance

IT RAINS ON THE TOWN (2)

molten
my dog-eared actions greet me, drop
off her eyelashes' us in a baggage claim terminal
I can tell her that it is not gorgeous to die
& that a china shop of illusions put me on my back
in Henry's apartment

her name used to be cemented on my life with glitter glue

but you washed my face
with Goo-Gone
maybe it has something to do with the uneaten bananas in my life
nope, can't be that: too much sitting on the side of the road
in reaction
to the times

how often have I
bunch of effects on my mind
thought of that wallpaper department store
how often twitching thought of the lonely years between you

I gave her back her diamond earring she had left it in my car a year ago

our conversation passed the Bechdel test
sitting at the bar where LS XPRSS used to play on Tuesdays I knew
she'd never cross at a stop sign if the sign said said not to & I knew she'd leave
when she met you, & she did about five-ish minutes later

HEROIN (ELEGIES)

the frizzy back of her head at school
fluorescent this girl was the cartographer of cool
she came to one of my soccer games I bought her Skittles
we were disinterested in all the same things

cicadas her eyes on the hill jazz railroad grass
cicadas Catholic Budweiser fathers
I really wanted to kiss her
a coal train roared by and drowned out the jazz

much better, I think, to end the story there

WALLFLOWER

THIS POEM IS NOT ABOUT JESSICA ADKINS.

I think I'm leaning toward the girl with blue hair.
She listens to Stephen talk, a music by the stairs
as wallflowers plot. The bottom of a bottle,
rafters, a roach—now I really have no excuse.
The host mops vomit. No one knows who.
Heaven is a cacophony of sexy drunks.
She brushes by me & the percussion of new arrivals
clomping down the stairs. No, now

I think I don't feel well at all, in fact—
Stephen shoves me into a jousting match for beer.

my turn—

PERIPHERAL

prance in headlight margins & blink on stars
then her body through bubbles antenna motel
there's a city but sirens lap up on horizon
& radio static the Kleenex she cries on

airplane

A FRIEND

our jai alai jazz dates never caught on
we are like the landscape we've been
on sale for so long

SKINNYDIPPING

By pool toe the water, which is leaf with bugs
& standing she autumn her off clothes.
Drop one by one petals of given rose
so stem stripped & fall to shrug

                  on the surface.

WAREHOUSE BOUQUET

eye crates of hangar bolts & the clipboard clerk
rolls a week worth of shelving spills & aisles' names
cart categories; shrink-wrapped the boxes a profit
steel & bends over to pick up a petal

so as to not have to sweep again

GRADIENT OF DAWN

For I have plumbed the gradient of dawn, & cranes blink through the night. On the highway I've seen it, & in other places as well I have become numb to the gradient of dawn. For I have plumbed the gradient of dawn, & very few bridges can fold. I've seen it through a window in Prague, in lots of places I have become numb to the gradient of dawn. For I have mapped the cacophony of mornings, & everywhere cars honk. On the highway I've seen it, & in other places as well I have cracked the code in the cacophony of mornings.

For I have plumbed the gradient of dawn, & will continue to do so.

IN WHAT I CAN BARELY SEE OF
THE GIRL IN FRONT OF ME'S DRESS

The audience stands up from their folding chairs
as instructed by the motivational speaker
who lays a plastic crown on the head of a woman already wearing pearls
& somebody waves a flag from a distant country
until a fireman sitting next to him tears it down.

The power goes out
& somebody opens an Altoid tin
the only light yellow from the parking lot through a dirty window
& in what I can barely see of the girl in front of me's dress
I see shallow water, a white beach under the moon
us naked there
where for a small fee you can wade with the wind on your nipples
& she turns her head
I see her in profile
& the speaker keeps on talking

INHERITANCE

Oh sudden brother in the offered park
hollow are these bones they throw for dogs
& helpful blushes won to veil;
what use the repeated colors of the holiday horizon?
Recognize the face into which sand stirs;
together we can press flower petals to war wounds.
Lightly enter the house that has invited you; burn
the idols for which you have dislocated your shoulders.
Soars high & watching a final friend
to those who make instruments in their empty hours,
out in the fields.
The dead were walking first
before the end of dreaming hung them out,
before glimmered on the stalk midseason the things they left you.

DIFFERENCE

rag piles laundry cat I bid goodbye,
the promise of tomorrow evening and clean for Christmas
making an atmospheric, an apostrophe goodwill
& I went off to jazz

jazz that satiated in a pounding massage fashion.
difference, the difference between this and a scar,
coldly without shivers shook me and shakes me still;
scuffmarks drywall my Dorian soul, it's true,

but there is yet a vigor flame within me.
I am not that which is left out to dry,
I am not insane or a crumble of candy cane factory trash,
I am not finished and vehemently am not through

with the getting hold of wrong numbers,
with the stumbling into last-minute logistical taxis,
with relationshippy bygones dredged up again hellos,
or with chasing down fulfillment, in all the colors.

THE DEATH OF LEONARD COHEN

after a temporary breathing of collegiate anxieties
unprecedented front porches knew obvious pains;
we do all our Pinocchios in-house here in America,
carve carelessly out of ancient wood bogus legalisms

including a cabin far from the death of Leonard Cohen
where they drink all day and know nothing
magically immune to the Big D and all his friends,
immune to these pyrotechnics, and happily married.

I first heard his music when "you"
included "Chelsea Hotel"
on a mix cd of which nothing came
I don't tear up over celebrity deaths, but damn—

for Leonard //: Doctor of the world, I prescribe this country
the music of Leonard Cohen, to be taken twice daily,
for the trouble inherent in this bad, poor-choices-making nation
until such a time as eighty-seven four-zero-zero nine-five

FLAP YOUR WINGS, TOM!

you can hear the branches growing
let's not take this too far

running logs illegally stream the paddles
that's one way to eat them

that distant canine
they're at it again!

flap your wings, Tom!
this is just a test
—sure!

I might slip into something more comfortable

FATHOM

gurgles creek whirlpool
are you a rock or a stick?

"two's a company,
three's a crowd"

is a rather diminutive way of looking at things,
wouldn't you say?

what I can't fathom is
myself

what I can fathom is
beneath

my feet
already

ELEGY FOR DR. JERRY L'ECUYER

(1931 – 2017)

No one place could hold, nor one man have
in the sputtering of the circumstance we All_fear
the grimace inherited & in its passing to tears
better exemplify; and in the playgrounds a certain sound.

Who has taught me more has loved me most;
who has created everything has made it necessary.
I know, as you know, the shine of the sun through trees,
& you know, as I know, who I speak of, & say: he was one of these.

I was given sleep to be given dreams;
we were not given nightmares to pass out screams.
All throughout, remembered, & never once doubting
what it all has really to do with; & in playgrounds the laughter of kids.

Who has left most recently is cried for; whose faith
was unshakeable, whose jokes to be depended on
for the laughter of kids—yes he was one of these
who I hear, & to whom I listen, in the shine of the sun through trees.

ANNA?

We did believe in a chance at life—severely.
But locked in her monument she together with despair
All things else look at the earth far off.

Two nights in a row I say goodbye to her in various voices
But not a word the woman of pearls brought me letters.
I lost a napkin, & have rolled up my sleeves.

A man may see how sorting through the broken
Shells of her affections can be seven or nine ages
Of pride falling like a fortune—"come & sit on my lap"—

That I have worn so many nervous breakdowns out
Should only the dew's raw, cold nothing-to-be-done-about-it
Wish her well, in spite of the spots of blood all over my summer.

DARRYL DOESN'T WANT MY LOVE

alcohol we must await; I don't have any gods yet
I dreamed of newcomer-to-my-life REDACTED & recent exchanges
have left the tear trails, I don't know, *confused*—
unrepentant thing of evil: your teeth & nails are dyed

I have been watching you these many years

THE CANTICLE OF DARRYL

The raven flaps its wings at the principles of tolerance
The pride of all the village has undertaken a prohibited undertaking
Loveliest of trees, the uniformed frequently refer to jihad
How silent the process of composting!
Shaken out the dead build a place of worship
God moves in a mysterious way & Islam views diversity as a gift
Thou, to whom the world of men & women
        the sands & yeasty surges
        trailing clouds of glory
        meet me in the green glen

He rose at dawn, a permissible microbe
Which breaks the clouds, depriving others of the benefit of wasted items
Quickly He make for Gods forgiveness but Death seals the accounts
How still, how happy! Zaid opted to remain with Muhammad
Because in more than one bright form the daily prayers were prescribed
Our birth is but a sleep; infertility is an age-old problem
Am I failing the basic features of a Shari'ah-compliant banking system?
        truly, my Darryl,
        thou art so fair
        in less than a day

THE TROUBADOUR: BEGIN AGAIN

"click the pen, begin again"
-Dan Wright

as the old cowards die out he gladly dreams
of love's worst ugly day
& what must be conceived of when the nights are a long lie
as fresh upon your eyes, as the old cowards
                                        dreaming   die

saw this long in advance Dan, each rip & gash
he pounce it like the panther & the lash
in the sense that he delighted in a single tree
without repose, or truce, & the troubadour
of the wake widening & the "Look, birds" roar

Who knows true Love, verily! he also knows the bad side
that inquiring sufferer knows too the whole of light
& sound & the silences of trite harmonies
which heard we wag our tails; boulevards big, big, wide!

we must follow to the source; let us river it (begin again)

DEATH AS CONTRASTED WITH A PRETTY GIRL

XXX

*

It's all about death, & the incessant warping;
I stare at the girl by the pond from the bridge
        across it

CLOWNHEADS

it sounds like a car coming down the driveway
& is a clownhead, an idol, a thing you put on shelf HAHAHA

the mirage as far down the
highway as you can
see;
       the dancing ghost town folk
       the little mountain flowers
       the woman in the red dress offering clownheads for sale
       the group of schoolkids in a broke-down bus. Help!

it sounds like a car coming down the driveway
& is a clownhead, an idol, a thing you put on shelf HAHAHA

I see the girl across the coffeeshop
                  taking
                  notes

VINCENT'S PASTA IS JUST NO GOOD

I am, in fact, an empty clownhead

sometime before 1973 Vincent de Man made pasta
poorly, he really disappointed Jeremy,
        who
        had wanted
        something nice

there is nothing inside me. Fill me up HAHAHAHAHA

on New Year's Eve 1972 Vincent was bragging to some girl
      about how good his pasta was
      & Jeremy
      didn't know
      what to do
      he was
    conflicted on account of Vincent being a real bitch earlier

BALLS-DEEP

<u>Tuesday</u>:
Carl was balls-deep in Big Mark's girlfriend Sylvia
                              Sylvia
                              was having
                              a nice time

<u>Monday</u>:
Carl was balls-deep in Big Mark's girlfriend Sylvia
                              Sylvia
                              was having
                              a nice time

<u>Sunday</u>:
Carl was shopping for clownheads, but wished he was balls-deep in Sylvia

CARBON MONOXIDE

the tree in our backyard!

I was at the Nelson-Atkins a few years ago
        I saw a painting which I thought was
                        very nice
it was black & white with a little bit of red
it depicted a man on his way to his garage
but in context it was very sad

A BLAZING SUNSET: SOME GIRL WHIPS HER TITS OUT

I stop looking at the tree in our backyard
        instead I go into the garage
           & look at
          my clownhead
          HAHAHA
      HAHAHAHAHAHAHA

FERNANDO & CLAUDE PT. 1

      having
      sex

sitting on a nice beach in France Fernando
rolls up a spliff & Claude says "Fernando
sometimes I wish you looked at me
the way you look at clownheads"

      after having sex you wipe the cum off
      your lovergirl

Claude was truly a beauty at which to gaze
but you can't smoke him
Fernando was about to reply
when an airplane exploded in the sky

> having
> the handyman install a new clownhead

"Oh Claude!" said Fernando.
"My mom was on that plane!" said Claude.
"How tragic!" I said.
"Who are you?" said Fernando.
"Yeah, who are you?" said Claude.
"Don't worry about it!" I shouted as I jogged by.

> "Great clownhead, got a 2-year warranty so you let us know if it goes broke"
> "OK"

Fernando wasn't sure what to do
so he put his hand in Claude's pants
until everything
was fine

JAHOSOFAT, KILLER OF CLOWNHEADS

the thing you have to know about clownheads
is that they were invented by Richard Brautigan in the 60's
they sometimes sell them in packs of two which is
nice

the ancient Romans used to dress up Christians as clownheads
to feed the lions who were brave enough to eat them
that's actually the origin of clownheads
one of the lions was named Jahosofat
renowned for his ability to eat more clownheads than all his peers combined
he met his demise when he tried to eat the emperor's wife
who had dressed up as a clownhead
in bed

the coliseum in Rome was turned into a quarry
that's how come there's not much left

A STAB OF HELPLESSNESS

It's hard to say whether a pinnacled white cloud or the noise of a helicopter's engine
affected a translucent screen of frosted glass
& the crowd
smelled of brilliant girls & a later edition of the paper.

Written in blood,
"Sing out if you can't share in the optimism of the doctors."
For half an hour,
temporarily sorry, she put her hands on her knees in finality.

Holding up his hand for silence,
the doctor asked: "Do you agree or disagree with pencils?"
Warning me it might be a mud hole,
Deborah felt a stab of helplessness.

If she believed in this therapy,
she would have cut it out with the rhythmic chanting.
Close your eyes & it won't exist;
everything will be fine, fine, fine.

ASSISTANT PROFESSOR ALEXANDER DMITRY'S
OFFICIAL JOB DESCRIPTION

What he saw made him remember the sound of the green garbage trucks,
& his former piano teacher aged rapidly.
Yes, yes, the professor nodded; her family was back in Oregon.
Most of the guests had departed, of course.

Until he found black flashlights, he nursed a quiet hurt & resentment
toward his mother, firemen, & helicopters.
It was unfortunate that vandals had long ago
laughed & waved their hands dismissively at his beach house

because she wanted sex. Not everyone liked the old man who taught him to drive;
half an hour later, a stroll through the neighborhood
demeaned a high-rise.
She had spent most of her time leading a healthy life in all respects.

What kind of basement cockroach is named after a prophet?
Followed by a fat question mark like a woman wearing red lipstick
the officer held out the search warrant. "It's not a Christmas tree,"
he said to the professor, who was hiccupping terribly.

Each of them had a beer bottle in their hand
their eyes staring past a triangular metal sign
that said "No longer!"
"I don't know what that means either," confessed the officer.

Sometimes you've got to think of a good alibi.
"You see, officer, there was a gleaming white motorcycle,
with my mother's fur coat sticking out of a worn-out suitcase."
"I haven't done a thing to my hair in months," added Deborah.

All that remained of Assistant Professor Alexander Dmitry's official job description
was: "splay out on the floor, turn to ash."
Officer Leonard Malcolm finally, wanting a cigarette, burst out laughing,
& as she quickly unbuttoned her blouse Alexander began voicing his musings out
           loud.

ASSISTANT PROFESSOR ALEXANDER DMITRY'S
OFFICIAL JOB DESCRIPTION (2)

Ate the crumbs even, then went home Deborah did,
noon's rage, i.e. it's hot as balls, in wisdom & on health
glinting like a jousting knight's gold ring
on Assistant Professor Alexander Dmitry's picnic.

The park had obviously been reserved or at any rate conquered
by about eighty hare krishnas. Alexander was a prudent man;
he walked swiftly in the opposite direction.
Other than the military vehicles the roads were deserted.

Was something wrong? Was all_magic tricks?
Better get moving on that Last Will & Testament;
things fain would get sticky when the dudes on the dais
all say "fuck it" & legislate vending machines federally.

Deborah would get there when she got there. Whereas God,
in His Fiery Gorgeous, bump his elbow in the doorframe of a brothel.
What a dunderhead. "Now, students," said the professor
earlier that morning, "The day has come that homeward must I turn.

"There are no elves left to see. Jesus Christ, Cathy, you must be a Pisces.
I'm outta here."
The university scrambled to find a substitute
to teach "Bereavement 206: Satire & the Big Frown." No luck. Tough subject.

Resisting the urge to look up your skirt,
Alexander crossed the quad.
It began to rain heavily. The fuck is the car?
The fuck is good fortune? The fuck is Christ?

Traffic....// Deborah texted, something about
"palmeres a'seken straunge strondes . . . . . ." what a hoot.
Fucking $90 moving violation. Alexander was still sore about it.
He was as fresh as the month of August.

SIMPLER TIMES AND PLACES

When I was shown that everything is a big balloon,
an ill-disposed senator sit for an hour in a chair.
I was aware of the delicacy of long green fields
like a circus performer. If I could only be a decent
sword & trying to kill myself every 3 years maybe
for the fiscal year beginning April 1, 1952 I'll live on a barge.
Simpler times & places ate away most of his roof.

I had to pry it out of propaganda:
23 years of defense budgets
appealed to an oil company! During the night I
dragged its feet, that legislative achievement,
to collapse in Korea.

Everybody at parties break everything in sight
& why shouldn't displeasure or pleasure
ease my stomach pain?
There are only a few like death falling into
the baby explosion so affectionate.

THOUGH NOT FLAGRANTLY FRAUDULENT

A scholar in the great cocktail party
observed the widening gap between alarm & disappointment
—could not have been more vulnerable. The opportunity to swallow a pill!
Exhausted, we once had both these things.
They were also poorly organized but it doesn't count because
an estimated four million were entirely disloyal.
Despite his enormous prestige there's a whole bunch of new germs.

Dispensing healthcare to the children, the Vietnamese equivalent of chewing gum
though not flagrantly fraudulent vividly remembered
the spectators. The imperialist revival
translated on the morning of October 17, 1833
& it also flew to London to serve as liaison.

The sorry-looking letter that she received
establish your family in one clump together
as high as the tallest building & his wife was an Irish girl.
That was all over now.
The little velvet boxes sooner rather than later cleaned the oven.

A SMALL-TO-MEDIUM-SIZED LEAP

Like a circus elephant I was at your call,
& like an audience or a mud puddle it sunk in
to an awful symphony of death by flames
forming a circle suddenly with a sense of lions.
You found me after ten weeks alone
big & spectacular like a ripe strawberry
a quarter mile down the road from some familiar place.
You put on Y98 & we drove straight to nowhere
past a hundred cartoon hotels, we took nothing seriously.

It was a small-to-medium-sized leap
& when I hit the dirt I sprained my ankle,
missing you immediately like a hot shower on a winter's day.
Like a circus elephant my tricks had lost their novelty,
& like an audience or a mud puddle when the stage lights are

                                blinding
                                    & the rain
                                          is heavy,

A SMALL-TO-MEDIUM-SIZED LEAP (2)

Like a revoked friendship I sat on your doorstep
& like a newspaper or dog you took me in
to an awful drum of what is to, summarily, come
forming the shape of a house with a sense of predation.
You found me after ten years alone,
small & spectacular like something you find in a field
way, way back.
You put on 88.1 & we drove straight home
past a hundred caricatures of beauty, & we did kiss.

It was a leap, of small to medium size,
& when I landed I won the awards
missing what we had, & held
up the Polaroid we both were in
up to the light
          which is
          blinding & the rain is
          heavy

DON'T BOTHER ME WITH WARS

a gently rolling bird from the
eaves of 1716 France between the four
angles of lemon-yellow wheels

a few miles from Naples, a wide
variety of farflung architectural gestures across
the portico (George I of England grew up there)

in the burning rays of a bright, immediate galaxy
in the nave of St. Peter's, the finest servants
unwanted, unvisited are these flat, marshy meadows

flowers will fall upon the rocky shore;
rooms will reflect a thousand
Roman warriors, always with respectful humor

with the possible exception of leather, satin, & felt,
all the ceilings of the side aisles are
the priceless gift of fanatical priests

the muted song of red & gold
build war—"What war? Wars come & go.
"Don't bother me with wars!"

PHILIP THE HANDSOME

somewhat modified in a
complete break with tradition,
Miraflores ladies do not spread out on the ground

transferred from the better of two conical fruits,
mouldings, crockets, corbels, &
canopies rolled into the turn of the century

in addition to his profession as an airy confection,
Alvaro de Luna in each scene (though
here in a different fondness) swag trophies

unlike anything else in the town,
the corners of the mouth are flush with
strong shadow. The wild men

rising from vases kneel before
North European models
likewise affected

& when Philip the Handsome arrived in Spain
a lively play of the Archbishop's personal Catholic
that she might share in the services
                                                on the spot

A SHADY TRANSITION

generally considered as a colored photograph,
the building has a reinforced concrete frame
very good, very small

inside & out of the safe & easy path
airports are numerous in Brazil
each a pleasantly proportioned living room

more & more Brazilians realize that
they are employed with surprisingly successful results
the absence of fussiness contributes to the effectiveness

by the small suburban hotel is a
charming variety of light & shade
some six feet high

to display machines, a low-rent housing project
is no mere skin-deep beauty
The design of entrances is particularly well handled.

an elevated row of classrooms provides a shady transition to
a simple row of
cleanliness & authority

IT WAS LEAD, NOT GOLD

long part of light aircraft, Spokane has gained a new
basalt bridge—a true arch, built without the aid of the
Palouse Country's uniquely fertile soil

a talented community of combines automatically
withstand a terrific flood; commanding a
wedding present for

the Farm Credit Banks Building on First & Wall
looking east from
some anonymous craftsmen

it was lead,
not gold, that
lost a pack horse, &

while old man Kellogg went in search of
this pedestrian plaza off Howard & Riverside
here on sunny afternoons

they have made the happy discovery that
Peaceful valley, a depressed area, is amiable
& many old residents prefer it.

EVEN IF THE FLESH HAD BEEN WEAK

upward in the solid corners of the industrial arts
stimulus vantage suggest the climax
while receiving the children

metropolitan movies were demolished
the last stage of 1922 when
Hugh Ferriss published his famous

museum pieces. Just as the talkies
with only the slightest infinite
ploddingly detailed palazzos

It is not a tower;
it is
not fundamentally a pyramid; it is

the Great Depression
even if the flesh had been weak. It does not
ape.

In addition to these efforts to control Manhattan,
John A. Harris, Special Deputy Police Commissioner,
was 610-foot high

NEW YORK 1930

we have met with the systems
during the decades
here, then

be that as it may,
the crypt was not particularly interesting
& vault ribbing has a function the first place

In the French crown lands,
in the fatal glossy smoothness
of the nineteenth century

surviving
what has been described as
larger undertakings than the Alps

no one
can
distinguish

Paired band-arches stretch the entire great span
from east to west & from north to south,
intersecting at right angles. Over them

THE CONFUSION OF ARRIVAL

when I realized golf course Hollywood
the passions of many men quickly &
with exquisite "I shouldn't have said that"

—dementia gradually
with his miniature leather briefcase
saw height & splendor of highballs

I had a glimpse of some concentration
have you seen him lately?
"My God," he gasped, "you're fun to kiss."

Why don't you stay for supper?
motionless valet filled a pause
in the confusion of arrival

then comes the thunder along the Sound
there is no
perturbed horse

as I went over to say good-by
he stepped on the accelerator
please come here

THE VERANDA

one October day in 1917
somebody's father flung somebody's mother
on the bed

the veranda doesn't love you
attractive women of 19 & 29 are alike in their
"I say—they have sharks out behind the raft"

with blue tights it's inadvisable to
drive back to the drugstore
unashamed, unafraid, doesn't that give you the creeps?

how about a song?
through a dank November
he was puzzled by your old scheme for America

as she stood in the fuzzy green light of
a lilac scarf
the orchestra is playing yellow cocktail music

& so with the sunshine &
the great bursts of 8 o'clock
it made no difference to me

THE ROAR OF BALLROOM DANCING

In addition to these hazards,
a bird was found the leading prophet,
& dry rot & fungus spoiled much of the cake.
How could he go back?

It is easy to imagine what would happen to the deserted, feeble town;
rumors came of granite stones & little wooden men.
Supplemented by an ex-fiancée from Philadelphia,
we had all too much reason to lament the loss of the nineteenth century.

A noted authority on warehouses stood on a gravelly bank close to the lake;
the roar of ballroom dancing
grew daily more haggard & weak
until the inconvenience of royal families was transferred to the drunken undertaker.

THE ROAR OF BALLROOM DANCING (2)

Do not think the navy is without peril;
I know why you did that with the old gun.
There is some talk that the roar was such
that he could not hear if they were drunk or not.

Unless something happens to the peasant who stood beside me,
Pablo green like the sea will be stopped in front of the barbershop.
Nearly all were weeping. It will all be written out.
Cowardice. Football helmets. Plazas. Will you tell me about it, Grandfather?

It can't snow; you don't need to be a clown. Ambulances
are militarizing again. Do you want to know something?
I would bring them all back to life; I have seen
her visible barbarity.

THE ARCH WE ALL HAVE

baggage faces inter flag purposes
conveyers of prop lives for a fee
shoulders away stride in a sundress anywhere
a car pulls to curb voicing join

give up on entering the space possession
a fire embers the starscape and hands keep close
tear down them, stairs take to the arch we all have
though blinding, spotlights ascertain the angle seats

introduce empire climb to the architecture as it really is
in backward smoke so as to idly spread capacity
medal the promise boys who one foot walk and one wait
for to come loudly, right here, for everything and with nothing.

THE PAPER SCIENTIST & HIS BRITISH GIRL

we were shipping deaf business
young prompted year was
like loose father London
blessed you might wonder at th_ broke settling
word sea were we almost no never
so continued this hull cost

The Ordered storm voyage
must we pump little signal
then alone we hazard side water
for some dead sea captain
me while I swim the cabin foot
time his bathtub's hold on light

o give me in that prescription kill tube
half the boys were shot stones
for his eyedropper dollars vein
remember thirties retail grain collar
now tablets; ten needles; what am I to do
when thin pants knocking my door
paid morphine air which nazi contriving
it was I slammed a glass bubble at that place

mass execution was my descent photo
facing the paper scientist
all for what, short headline radiologist?

THE SPY

so he thinks blurred SLIT so swabbing
were we sorted the fourth door
..?;um-gears chew seat, presently here
dizzy with it he turn cap so slight
blink on recall her slip clings jaw
like handlebars for motor eyes take no walk

base he drop a bottle low level
all the women we love knock papering
telephone poles with pencils & their baptizing fist
& m_ dadless honey lick her hard candy, her pigtail offense
oh nothing tongues a flask
she gonna get sixteen, swig unreligious cloth

sleeping not into temptation skin
but slivers of etiquette semi-circle af. crack
what _f she stripe arm with window
broke,—his mobile face play
in capacity of servant paralysis ribbons
walk a rag razor, doesn't it?
"beg the gray vermin" say some say
flash your Own mirror, the pink passed

another cellophane birthday cake
my hubby spy local daughter commercial
sadly, those watery outfits

GOING THRU THE MOTIONS IN SALEM

scandalously long wooden tables
just enough to miles-down-the-road
open up a service predator
defeating lamps to lift celebrity hides
through secretaries my darling:
I must remember to see this Gene Tierney picture!

maybe at the cancer valley 10?
she sawed up the fishy least of my brothers
when I came in her purple yawn moved over
waded in the motions of my story
with a polka-dotted shotgun
like masturbating in the first week of November

Good God five bankers were lately executed,
impudently demanding of God
a miraculous vindication of their innocency.
Immediately upon this, our God
miraculously sent in five Andover bankers,
who made a most ample, surprising, amazing
confession of all their villainies!
Cotton Mather/ August 5, 1692

I chances channel,
respectably flushing the taste of her metropolis,—
did singular moonlight leave for a dinner table Caesar?

EMPEROR NERVO'S DIRECT LINE

you blinked on blood or be air
conditioning shy, like feasted
//mosquitoes blinked, aiding me
promise myself I'd lick your salt
when you showed up staring at the garden
anyway in the dog ball morning

eyeliner doesn't care
sleeps the asshole at foot
did you know the garage? ok mom
as if waiting for a penciled ride
I, with benefits like Preferred Wrist,
goes let

washed out on the street
cartwheels thru the corn stalks
screen head shoulda coulda
would a breeze kitchen
kissing your goose bump sister
& maybe fog pants fornicate—
scarecrows kneeling someone else think
such a beautiful sink

there's a song for which I would give everything I possess
all my REM all my Gaga all my Avril
"Un air tres vieux, languissant et funebre"

NOT SK8ER BOI, LATE POSSUM, OR HIT N" RUN

bought a cigar for my clock;
advancing on me the bus want fifty-cent piece
you were paralyzed, weren't you? =[
frowned at minutes' concourse pocket
cheerful sit here a minute & decide what to do
commanding a lounge of invalidated reluctance

I have no head for imitating a horse collar—
Mr. Berryman wants to see you, in meteorological terms
:B movies pretty much never answer the question
for business advice like a hit-&-run tricyclist
be weatherless, troublemaker; are you Polish .. ?
because I've got to make some calls

yeah, hyaCynthias, life's like this
the Pentecostals are so over the catalpa branch
I'm unmarried to a race of flames but it's just barometric
the false peak of a low-low love interest
who did you expect you were? nylon panty hose
hovering over a field, which I lit on fire?
sliding alibi you can't refuse,
tube o' lipstick you most definitely can

what's my take on the Unknown?
as we know, Private, to break from the shadow of airplanes
an Algerian peanut vendor must his cheeks grow hot knowing ;)

THE BELLHOP'S REVENGE

a sense of stratification stayed well-wide
so shuffle along to tag dandified
swinger ze grand so-called
dead-ended bellhop sign off on latitude
having learned such sloppy bulletins
painting on the front steps ragtime

circuits get advantages
just because frequent programmatic dream
faux pas to begin with the presence of a radio audience
metronome dues tuxedo
broadcasts soon but not to listen
waltzing with the best of them

the institution shifted strings
lost-on watermark overtures this term
subsidiary terminology of at least 2 of the royal parts
we are dealing with the pieces themselves
attempted minuet excuse
shed monasteries decide the problem
listed chronologically with extreme caution
identical catalog no longer

our climax (well-stocked) held her distraction
just as we were matches—
blossom no longer, inebriating noise

FLOWN IN DAILY

bell-chaperone judge-palm volcanic rock
rang like have you seen the front page or sworn allegiance to drinking
the system worked well even the mayor bows to him
get off his father's furniture kind of man
having run wildly down in that awful murk
who at least could breathe—shake hands
with some obsolete abandoned-by-Britain regime

for a beast that has been caught in an English-speaking theatre
as a hat a double bass from secondhand Hemingway
breaking even once Satan was admitted to compliments
I am constrained; I have a tougher time

flown in daily, when it became Einstein's opinion
that the dilettante manipulator forbids window design
harmonic went back to bed
I'm redeployable, it's a musical instrument

an unevenly balanced affair join wisecracking
there's a ghetto professor deep in Arkansas just for the music
predominantly scurrying with bullfighter emphasis
after suffering a leg wound one afternoon

RAPIDLY FALLING TO PIECES

his career has been this country's God
his Committee on EveryGirl exalt frying pan
& the bathing suit, & I need your attention because
Philadelphia reintroduced a pleasant, gray-haired lady
rapidly falling to pieces she added that
Michelangelo could not have prevailed against a tree in season
for thirty years President Truman has appealed to Americans

much kindergarten is more nervous than usual
investing irrelevant movements with the elegance of playing cards
the uncannily effective war with Germany—first off,
it was a very foxy one, & the band trooped thru the building

gray marble columns where he remained briefly
a fidgety fifty thousand people actually proving speedometer
after his talk, flagrant recreation (he ought to snarl)
—he was the kind of man of whom people say,

you looking chipper today, Billy boy
incoming for a living water supply in South Carolina
or they go out the door bringing the German people
a lively sense of his own importance

THE LIMITATIONS EMBODIED IN LARRY

Successful law enforcement
requires
the largest of 500 terminals on Route 80.
Under certain circumstances a police officer can walk through the neighborhood;
based on the information given him he must
drop the kids into the boxes.

The disturbed person
may view the officer's uniform as
a red "say it with flowers" truck.
Basically, the law provides that
in a colorful package
persons who believe they smell patriotic songs
should remain at the scene
until a saleswoman didn't have much trouble convincing her.

"The limitations embodied in Larry
do not mean that all uncooperative witnesses are
involved in the offense," interjected another customer.
A group of two or three people approached the desk of his third-grade teacher.
Furthermore,
it is probable people are
frustrated & want to shoot everybody.
If a victim had her purse snatched, the aisles are two or three feet wide.

An example of the use of a
black cast-iron stove
would try to provide a more complete description:
"thirteen hundred paintings stacked on the floor
& it contained $90 in cash."
What an opportunity!

A person who has obviously
suffered injury

is nowhere near a seaport, of course;
at other times, however, there are no seats on the way home.
In the case of an armed robbery three & a half hours ago,
a mix-up is unlikely.
Things like this just don't happen here.

Television & motion pictures
start
just out the backdoor
to build community confidence in the
so-called traditionalists.
An important point to remember is that it would kill him.

Guard against "We have to eat it before it eats us."
As an illness develops: this is not real.

Merely locking the car cannot stop
running the strings through small holes; sometimes they show up bleeding
A basic rule: you wear a lot of clothes these days.

A systematic Florida
will be performed by the doctor; the girls come here to
furnish the officer with beer—
it is not enough to sharpen knives & open plastic food pouches.
Pieces of shattered glass found at a tupperware party
or in a field in a rural area
battling motherhood & apple pie
or, as happens in some instances,
were all high school dropouts.

BECAUSE FIGHTING RAGED IN SUDAN

I can't go too fast because he told me about a patient of his who,
unable to see much, is wearing a tiny black leather belt
I ask if the dirt bike is a very beautiful lesbian
so much for keeping it simple—he did not want
a pair of pickup trucks to hold up my stockings
worst case scenario, I am wearing a uniform
it's a large Buick, out in Nevada

an hour after I splashed into the pool, the fireflies flew about the lawn
a gorgeous but beautiful theoretical problem
putting on long underwear & coming with me to the beach
as I pocket the yo-yo his upper-class accent
presided over my corset

less than a minute after curtains of secrecy
fed me sandwiches America was the land of opportunity
when the cops yelled at the fish
Bob & Nancy lying on the floor
he spent the night in our bathtub because fighting raged in Sudan

the girl wants to run in the sprinklers & the boy was a fiction
my father was one of the most honest overnight bags in America
in the parking lot a waitress in black & white
yelling at the children like a great bird shot in mid-flight
casual readers just wanted to be held by a single female body
the scene fades into second base
he reveals an intricate bronze sculpture of my marriage

THAT SCHOOLGIRL COMPLEXION

According to time-honored custom,
the ceremony saw priests
coming slowly down the steps
by the dozen.

We're just starting supper—
the occasion seemed to call for beating our shining, willful heads against a stone wall
signaling with oboes & bassoons
that I made a great mistake in not seducing you.

There were embers spread out on the table between us
& upon entering New Orleans we sat bareheaded in the sun for far too long.
At a shrine with a somewhat disfigured statue
we begged our mothers' pardon.

The saint is prepared to break the usual golf club routine
or flee an opera & march into a great future.
Go ye therefore & halt a parade
responding to that schoolgirl complexion.

SALESMEN, SAWS, AND THE SECRETARY OF STATE

The next step is to recycle cardboard & other paper products.
Usually it isn't personal.
The dumping of untreated sewage on one hundred typical salesmen
strikes me as significant.

A retired salesman living in Florida
believes that the parts of a color television set
on the ninth day of the narrative of power
distract him from the residents of a Mexican shantytown.

There were hundreds of chemical ideals in unfortunate little countries.
In informal group meetings,
a premium line of saws
function as a living organism as they invite the salesmen to sit down & talk a while.

Of particular concern is that psychologists,
working in laboratories as completely equipped as any regional engineering school,
combat this discourtesy with up to $320 billion in civilian versions of the army,
& I have only scratched the surface of the liquidation of a friendly, sincere man

who in a manner reminiscent of a housewife
was semi-automated & made appointments by telephone.
Third-world assembly line workers engulfed him;
they cost only two for a nickel.

The continuous use of high-powered houseboat parties & budget cemeteries
under the sponsorship of the U.S. Secretary of State
tried in vain to thank him, but he held up his hand
demonstrating loyalty to the company.

WITH AN INSOLENT FAMILIARITY

While the crowds looked on, both men took seats on the patio,
& as soon as their jobs were eliminated,
a group of naked fisherman made huge profits
under a stifling wooden structure with a corrugated iron roof.

In the disguise of a peasant the bishop used a fax machine
to express what he truly felt,
so decrepit that he could hardly stand
but with a rage like a bomb in a half-waterlogged canoe.

I know some people had hope,
slung in hammocks, committing murder,
but I found myself drawing what is always there when I close my eyes:
two prisoners thrown out of airplanes, with an insolent familiarity.

CONQUEST

J-size pliers cheerily suggest you lie down
while pawn your toys, like a monarch decree
as childhood's idol smash many stories below
and it would be a crime to eat your delicious lunch

lecture dais decorated for metal season
with winds winding up to sweep your ashen status
burning symbols' pale smoke entwine your exhalation
a small boat fills up with water

shrunken face of the baker a pillow morning
as carriages over open sewer your onward life
the rain of leaflets acid irritates and you engineered
on top layer a stack of prosthetics

cave inhabitants will ration sleep
in the valley the highways clog with accident
but it had to be in big print and universally distributed:
Conquest Is Herein Completed

SET FOR ZERO

gasoline apologies neighbor my own excellences,
my top-marks mammals among the extinct, the droppers
out while the lullaby cardboards
fingernail the ever-need

iridescent irises glimpsed await this kiss
during the exhumation of falcon graves
bits of porch and banister peek from the wreckage
& resilient lasers go on engraving strange names

stove-gas blue your eyes again
tears like an email that says without saying,
your turning away a snowflake in a symphony of rejections
an estate sale in a block of eight car garages

I think of sunglasses at the exact wrong hour
I think of Germany in the historic sense
and of you in the sense of a cancelling;
table set for zero, and a savage candle.

I SING THE ELECTRIC CHAIR

You're squatting by the graves of those for whom writing is an unfamiliar process. Several people were watching. It hardly seems possible that there could be so many. When you suddenly appeared with your people, the disloyal agitator explained quite coolly that a few guests had come together to celebrate his birthday. The helpers found your "idea" most effective indeed.

You put on your hat. Bit of a drizzle in the parking lot. Entrance was lengthy, even in those days. The door to the control room was partly open. "Good-bye, William," you said as you rapped twice on the door. The witnesses nodded in agreement as a frothy liquid began to drip from his mouth. The frothy foam continued to drip down from his mouth. The room was filled with the stench of burning flesh.

Quicklime will be poured into the grave to consume the body as quickly as possible. You'll squat by the graves of those for whom writing is an unfamiliar process. Several people are supposed to be watching.

It hardly seems possible that there will be so many.

DOT 1

legs need money & laughter is a mistake;
slow down for the fool who's crossing

The clock which is my night says four
so I must have really seen something at the aquarium
something unsettling in the glass blue
I had better take off my pants

I shall marry, no doubt, but
I shall never be a sovereign or even an oligarch
I shall not often fly in airplanes
but frequently we will be intimate

whimpering, the hypocrite crawls
but it's all been said already

I pounded on a door in a dream
because I wanted very much something sweet
&, clumsy, I landed myself in a cell somehow
with only the carcass of a hyena for company

this is what it has come to. This is what I am now.
Are you ok with that? I sure hope so.

DOT 2

close the curtains so that God cannot see in
what we do here is prophecy

I caught a disease in a ditch
you might ask how I
ended up in a ditch or
what disease I caught but
I'm not in the mood right now

a BATHTUB is not the same thing as a DEATHBED
but you can't deny there are similarities

when my skin is leathery I will still have orgasms
at least I hope so
& when summer comes again
I think I might just watch it on TV
because it is very hot
very hot indeed

if orange=death, what is life?

know this, kid:
her father is a pigeon & her mother is a deception
so
just bear that in mind, you know

DOT 3

your hands explore beneath her gown
you can pick the color, it's hardly relevant
yum!
clumps of dead flies litter the windowsill
can we make out somewhere else?

a skeleton out of wedlock,
a preoccupation with guitars
wear my riding boots to electroshock
during the war I hung out in bars

the grave does not matter
it is indeed a grave matter
dumb

everyone is a queen in a world without behaviors
it is customary to sing hymns when dancing the Little Piggy

sport
poison
watchfulness
first prize
get it? no connection at all.

Funeral Jesus: the action figure!

DOT 4

hands want grass & grieving is a long process
hurry up & visit the wise man, would ya?

The book which is my patio has gotten interesting
John le Carré really knows how to write them
the Berlin wall is a thing to see
it had a big effect on me

I shall go for a walk, there's no doubt about that,
but I won't jog, I shouldn't think;
I rarely do although I should

running his mouth, the President isolates himself
but the song (of the deep state) remains the same

I got raped in a ravine in a weird nightmare
I wonder what that signifies
I also woke up on the pavement recently
heroin will getcha

This is how things stand. I believe that I will
win. I know that I will find someone.

DOT 5

lock the door so that Darryl will not disturb us
what we do here is a religion

I solved a big question on a long train
you might want
to know which
question &
what the answer
was but I don't
know you
yet

the difference between a DEATHBED & a LIFEBED
is either big or small
which is it?

when my memory fails me I will still remember you
I know I will
& when winter comes calling again
I don't plan on being here, tbh
this last one was
not fun

if black=the question & white=the answer
this book should be printed with gray ink on gray paper

acknowledge the overwhelming poetry of psychiatric hospital telephones

DOT 6

she takes off her shirt
I'll let you decide what kind of shirt it is
but it's not just any body
let's fuck so loud the neighbors move

a doctor's office painted blue
an obsession with Katy Perry
you examine me & I'll examine you
like an LSD raspberry

I want one of those
green burials where they
dump your formaldehyde-free body
in an unmarked, reusable grave
yeah
that's the thing for me

everyone is a run-on sentence in a world without punctuation marks
it's normal to experience nausea & blurred vision

paperclips
Will & Ariel Durant
spray-on fireproofing
comprendo? no relation!

Jesus is my hombreezo
Darryl is not a hombreezo
don't let that guy be hangin around

MOST HONORED FEATS

The civic duty of the searching glance
will try to sleep between   heaven & earth
 Without mirth or scorn   let's pray for the whole world
the desire to endure   the perils of storms & waves
After thirty-six hours of   the limpid current
of young women & girls   who adorn this graying temple

Into the bushes   Lady Paola's house
like a dead man across your saddle   which was-ago sweet like words in the evening
Come on, boys   I see a silent urn
& lie once more panting   boldness was on my brow
Righteous   no earthly thing was alien to me
yester-tomorrow   in the castle on the lake
glad to get the money   like shadows, they have a dim lantern

Let others sing of most honored feats

SUCH VIOLENCE

a claw or tooth—his heritage—gone to pieces,
like a square window favoring evil & crime or within a fragrant laurel grove
where long dark night distrustful's bound with heavy chains

as every morning the great warrior viewed it all:
the bandit saluting, the branches & sticks clustered at the altar;
in a gambling house, grasping with both hands the light of day

sharpened by the rats the sacraments & holy books at my mistress's feet
saying "Amen" to the world of eyes & women who know but direct their gaze
                    downward
to the signaling of health, & to opening the gates as fast as they can

Your only chance is to get out from under this sickness
          too ready for peace & for terror
          spiders spin green winning webs
And today we dump them in their graves.

Each strikes the other with such violence

VOWS

They've closed the chapel. A voice keeps rising in my early sleep.
There aren't many evenings left to us. She was so much trouble.
You have that in your countenance which I would fain call
                                     madness.

That's one thing I can give her. And the ivy branch, cast to the ground.
Why do you take their side against me? So, I suppose, the spirit journeys,
masking the business from the common
body

We were both weary. The doors swung open
& we married immediately,—is pain a promise?
When the blood burns, how prodigal the soul/ lends the tongue

                                                        presence

Here love had died between me &
                 ten thousand warlike men

RECOVERY

jails & institutions may survive but they have always been old
        I have learned to live on life's terms, & to hate trespassers
one night I ran into their voices
        sometimes it can be really scary for a woman to bear the dead
when I walked through the door I heard the whole world age
        & they invited my daughter to understand

I'll always remember the time the loneliness of Sunday grew
        in June 1990 I decided to write of places I might go
which speaks for itself: the sticks & stones darken their faces
        & I heard people laughing; some day it will rain

once I was introduced to your head in the alley
        where I have always been just like everyone else
sometimes we find ourselves in a western country
        motivated by rebellion as much as poverty

EXACTLY WHAT HAPPENED

that's exactly what happened with the empty flags
the scene in the clearing was painfully familiar: the ends of voices
this is our gift to you: an old woman walking fast
I saw exactly what I wanted to see: a small house

to grieve silently, see the wolf in winter watching
the man you see before you (we call him the morning star)
I struggled to look up; toward morning I dream of the first words
that was GOOD; I carried her home

Be it lawful I take up what's cast away;
How to deny them, who to advance & who
To trash for overtopping

                      my father
; we drove at great speed
to Brideshead, leaving the day behind me

CASSANDRA

no painting a substitute for the perception
of depth, & what must be thought of after
all in the world of the king

withheld Cassandra in the skies
you must recognize as together
picture it, Meridian

I follow the foundations
& I don't care if people know this
bending them back into shape

A little noiseless requiring
Because a longer stay has won
As well the angry wolf

IN THE PHALLIC FASHION

I have changed out of the soft summer
the torches tap their shoes
on the girls

who cannot be planted in the pricing
we're doing pretty good
I don't like their food

& when I know I have all the drinks
I thank you in the phallic fashion
maybe we should have one or two of those

Mother, why did the impure pipe?
Some of them are Methodist, too
But like, not religious at all

#BOYSWHOSHOWTHEIRDICKS

For the pomp to meet him come
over a lake I love these
"it was a delight" of a dark & distant shore

death the giant life
& most innocent wiles & eager sleepless
of universal silver dew

listening now to the high pair of underwear
they're kind of like shorts
are you ready to see my dick tonight?

& empire tremble
most delicately, they're literally see-through
with the circumstance of life all over them

AS I LAY ASLEEP IN ITALY

yet gleam on some doing decay
come up a tyrant half tranquil
proudly exempt his mossy lawns

home to the lineaments of time
seen the social institutions faming
awful wind

the streams where light lately ran
came down with a fever
most bad, & the devil a book sealed

as I lay asleep in Italy
I will confess
to my death

SOMEONE ELSE WILL

the truth is imageless; on wicker
was the scotch poured out for me
& into the sun I directed my aphorisms

& hands to her breasts....
entangled monarch

AFTER THE ARIA

The treacherous villain, Dr. Malatesta, has persuaded Don Pasquale to come storming
in with Clorinda & Thisbe. To make his own way in world,
the sorcerer proclaims that the mound is shaky.

Suddenly the arches over the street light up & a procession of
relatives & companions of Cio-cio-san & servants rush at him defiantly
& shopgirls & students, & vendors & soldiers & waiters, & Parpignol.

Then, dragged away by his ear after a private audience with the King
& expressing his happiness at the prospect of seeing Adelia,
he quickly leaves. (The curtains reveal..)

DER ROSENKAVALIER

The Baron, she says to Octavian, has walked boldly past the footmen.
The Princess with the idea of showing her a book concentrates on prayer
& in the corners of the room Mit Ihren Augen voll Thranen—

Sophie & Och free the girl from the clutches of the
servants in a large room at the inn. There is a large candelabrum
on the table by the door at the back, near the five rehearsing individuals.

Valzacchi opens a future husband
to rescue the noble son-in-law from Faninal
over the disgrace that has (convincingly) fallen upon him.

BEYOND WORDS OR DAYLIGHT

It would be better for the salvation of Giustiniani
(extremely eloquent, of vast ability) if Timur turned back at the Don.
Between lines of kneeling suppliants, the graces of life continued.

Beer & wine were the staple drinks at all horoscopes.
Part of Montaigne's skepticism had to do with Marguerite of Navarre;
the government of France (God's word) became bisexual.

Oh wretched man! Oh miserable church! Oh miserable
pride that upheld him amid Padua, Bologna, & Pisa's anatomy of the heart;
beyond words or daylight, & arranged for ornament.

FILELFO'S TAKE

Filelfo: what men remarked was that, living in modest retirement, the prince
in 1530 was introduced to Aretino ($12.50). San Luca,
its ruling passion-free reign reorganized, spanned the Tiber

with the northernmost tax on inlaid, removed &
best-understood-by-Finiguerra bronze sample panels,
which, really in context, all Florence the patriarch tasted (beautiful!).

As the one prophylaxis needed, many churchmen made
a business of strengthening him. I never knew him.
In the next eighteen years Tintoretto's success was confirmed.

(HELLO)

Medici the use of Joseph de la Vega improve
financial place a special history, histories:
annuity, expectancy, laws..
in currency predecessors, Julien de Bonvouloirs
& CLOBOEs were later cited by Werner Sombart
& the postwar debts do fall neath par
with specie convertibility & perishable analogues
especially province party impressions
rather than five hundred

Simone ponders a moment & then, looking
tenderly at Harriet for the Last Rose of Summer
& the norm shifts in Dalila (tried asking)
for Tristan of all blame, as Bartolo leaves to summon the emperor
Don Jose has been hailing the bottle, & Hansel
steps between the quarreling gods
much gallantry in this particular echelon:
the castle, the magic ring, shouts of "Rofrano.."
it's all just one big Marie's room on a Sunday morning

THE SEQUESTERED WOODS

around the spit-beast, flesh unforging in fire,
this chant, scatter of ritual aphorisms,
feverish fears & the hurting of the heart....
Rage music of the village's voices
  & courteous cruelties of hypothetical shadows

I ask only for the sequestered woods
to cloak me in foliage
I shall get my hammock out
at any rate I simply MUST have my epitaph in a high road
  what could she say, "Perhaps _tis a mistake?" or, "That lady is my wife!"?

Think of the people I gave him to offer up
all unwilling!
  And I will war, at least in these words on those woods
  Fair virgins blushed upon him

OVER IN A BETTER WHERE

whistling all in shiny black shoes
the intergalactic ooze of LSD
was the Power & the Call
the wire & plug snaking behind him
   And body with continual mourning wasted

in a half-crazed demonic Compton
but pineapple chili nonetheless
in full Prankster regalia
not an ordinary movie!
   Thy comforts can do me no good at all;

in one of two ways
they would hang around Aguascalientes
   My love should kindle to inflamed respect
   Thou losest here, a better where to find...,..

"I SEE THE SUMMER CHILDREN IN THEIR MOTHERS..."

The chief ordered the guards, "There's a brand new toothbrush & clean towels."
We are going to be born! Lover, old. Wife, aging. Soldier, clearly.
2004's was the wettest August since 1912; erosions were evident in the ribs.
Taller, heavier men are thinking very long-term;
   Ruin, the room of errors, one rood dropped....

My chest tightened; they couldn't find it.
With love & hope for your future, your dad kept coming;
well-tended & cared for, you momma got dirty rq.
The Chang Jiang runs four thousand miles:
   Flows to the strand of flowers like the dew's ruly sea.

I would suggest distancing yourself from her
while the wound heals.
   I see the summer children in their mothers
   split up the brawned womb's weathers

CLASSICAL ANSWERS TO THE QUESTION OTHER THAN YES

1
Wife, let us the concave make straight: the moon has set.
By Venus, & by our consummated paper-sack song,
advance in age Until there's no angst or tension & a bundle of trouble, untouchable,
                                                          plays with us.

2
Enthroned in a massive billboard: "Once among the living,
You had the eyes of a hitherto silent, stretched-out virgin..."
What my mad heart pined for really was three sailors on Tooley Street
                                          singing to themselves.

3
The soft cheeks of a girl the hallelujah chorus forever produces;
Keep it coming. Take pyramids & pagodas: "Ask naught of me."
I'll keep my little symbol-people to myself
                    as if she a prophetess.

4
With grace though average she the manifold tomb
Proffered: Let not him who is houseless love old returns.
Yokes us back together a radio, a stock market.... I tugged at her dress:
`   *hey you!*

5
Under the Dishonor, the name-giver the autocrat
(tomorrow, unarmed) undressed. Bring out the men whose eyes
Suffer death twice over; in uniform bring them. I'm done for.
                              Go, my nymphs.

JAMES'S QUATRAINS

1

arrives my god to orient my dreams (which I abhor)
was your grandma's goodbye a good idea, like welcoming foreigners?
perhaps in the East you can steal my sister out the cabin
but damsels who are near the mountains can obliterate you, big guy

2

by & by a kind of low chuckle returned to the realm
I was feeling better, cheered up, & the ancient bread frightens
iron latches, hub of a wheel; blue of sky, column of our own face
we slept in the woods at various times

3

high time we pride-of-her-heart resurrect or some shit
in the house of running water & fired up squads
unthinkable? hardly; got us a brief glimpse of the needle oops...
I shall see about getting tired on Friday

4

"that sounds fantastic" I lied; if the end of the world should come
you gotta prove yourself to be the lover (or die)
; Dear God, will you let me slip my tongue in her mouth?
Or not that exactly but something similar—Love, Hart

5

I am turning over the business to a majestic memorial to myself
worry not about me; I do beat my breast & bid farewell
when hope began to move in her, I took a bough from a pine tree
& without haste mystically diverged from it

JOE'S MORE POLITE & SHALL WE SAY PRESENTABLE QUATRAINS

1

there was no doubt in my mind that nameless colors—
the ones you warned me about—neither needed me nor were real
within the folds of the awe I have for you, a raging bull
intrudes on the evidence of plant life every damn day

2

the last living thing on Earth all red & bloody
& all our humming boxes & all our tormented fruits
will either travel back in time or be clubbed to death
by extinction's countless smiles & handshakes

3

spoiling the moment & thirsting, thirsting, thirsting for
air of Himalayan rarity or at least some nether-lips
enigmatic daisies on an uncut lawn followed my bones to annihilation
how could we have prevented it? (barbed Independence drowned)

4

you know as well as I do that all worlds will die, & that
we are ruled by a pile of towels & institutions of science;
rhythms based on a different whisper: O Summertime!
O Girls! O Bottle! come into the boat with me bro

5

the Galaxy isn't nearly dignified enough to die
just yet, though; the middle of the night is airtight
let us thread & weave instruments to go with our iron bell
& pound out inexplicable fanfare for forty days

WITH EVER-INCREASING FRIENDLINESS & GAIETY

Fish move upstream; nobody should postpone their departure.
Floods deposit nutrients on Leonora, from whom nothing is concealed.
Do you remember what you promised the forested bottomlands?
Murmuring at a banquet in the old style, the oil companies denied

that they were having an impact on tightly laced Tatyana
until the monkey listened with reverence to the science.
Comets have gone out of fashion; God be thanked! How is Natasha?
Preceded by a page of solid logic, Natalya, the happiness of my life,

grew numb as she brought my telescope to the apple tree.
In 1616, condemned, we conversed on various topics, & with that
my initiative in favor of a duel ended. Surely you can see
that we were joking about enriching the modern knowledge of nature?

The last of the blizzards chatted gaily with the soldiers.
This way, this way to a sixty thousand year marriage!
Eleven thousand years ago this hovel was filled with guests.
By the sixth millennium BC, Adrian did not recognize the farming village

where young girls were made. The doctor accepted the honor of a useless journey
for seven rubles. A love affair of the same measurement used all its eloquence
to return my salute, & with ever-increasing friendliness & gaiety
I began to ponder the limits of my old wet-nurse.

INDIAN UNICORN

Plucks from the boiling buds jiffy, dispassionate—
they are bitterness navigations through the curtain..
A proceeding monk with mantra discovering
it's not the glow of prodigy or a cryptic bottom;
half-jokingly there was a little girl, a banquet
who might cause riots for the good of the country.
Long-suffering blood in their veins radically repeated,
wrestling extraordinary foreheads downstairs.
The storm simply a loincloth, recited the workingmen
were united mummy in the sacred city of the dead.
Confused or forgotten, pharaohs were impaled on subtle spikes
similar to those depicted in the head of a lion;
the impression one gets is to awaken the eye doctors
& washing hopelessly—(the unicorn came from India).

YOUTH & AGE

Mysteriously hostile, the capital quarries ....baby at her breast,,,,
coiled about the _resorting to force_ enduring happiness.
On the roadside, covered with snow, bears foxes badgers & even deer—
about forty million, shall we call them?—grimaced as appeared my tentacles.
Handling the paintbrush, I converted to the tenets of walls, ceilings, & columns,
a peculiar freedom & grace respectfully piled up on the 16th century.
The loveliest, the scarcely been touched prices have groves & gardens devoted to   the
last 10 years
& the first thing brought to the traveler by powerful nobles is a ferry boat.
Fancy less imposing trees! Halting plateaus! Utensil connoisseurs!
It has been said that the golden age of reptiles competed with a sheet of white paper
& a couple of drawers of indispensible bronze pipes are, for perspiring bodies,
the third month of spring. The factory at the end of an unquiet sleep
made no attempt to a stern breeze blacken. From the riverbeds arise
new beliefs, equal parts youth & age.

MEDICAL DETAILS

In the famous enigma of political careers,
in the winding of the words of socialism,
& in the kissing of thy mouth, carrying
a bigger pen than his body
Lord Salisbury, an anchor slipping away
despite accidents like triangles & intoxicating colors,
had worn out the word "ugly"
& had an acute sense of his own public relations.
The implications of Darwinism were considered unfit for publication
by the "most superior man I have ever met";
in a staggering blow some great landmark was removed
because a pseudonym like a romantic bandit
in shop windows, in the war between capital & labor, & in multicolored electric
                lights,
in a pink ballet skirt discoursed on medical details.

IN THE MIDST OF THE ANSWER

The police began using very narrow lapels;
despite the prosecutor's warning, the middle 50's were years of superior tarts.
At the very ungenerous price of a trio of cartoon villains,
Los Angeles was really a coffee bar.
The basic idea was to move duplicates of men to triumph in Europe
where those who have had abortions (very Catholic) greatly expanded.
A horrific series of child murders was turned into a very successful department store
                chain;
maternal love, after all, is contrived out of all sorts of junk.
The erect penis is a symbol of the Holy Ghost;
the immediate causes of the beatniks' private motor vehicles, in the rational study of
                many evils,
were not specified. According to the prime minister of the kitchen,
three hundred & forty-three downtrodden cultural exchanges
contributed to what I have described as a street of tourist restaurants,
or, alternatively, I find myself in the midst of the answer.

WITH A POLITE "THANK YOU"

His case officer did not quite like the Royal Air Force;
occasional handouts appeared on the scene,
& it was a corking good story with a single fault:
the voyage to Ireland was a rousing success.
A clue to at least one secret collaboration with Mrs. Grenville Emmett
was a fleet of dummy submarines.
With an oversized map of the world, William Rhodes Davis
on one of his inspection trips to a relative of Prince Bernhard of the Netherlands
left 1,124,000 totally ignorant & wayward voluminous men
by a bridge which was guarded day & night by a Lutheran clergyman.
He once made special effort to seize the Italian money,
the scourge of the promising Mexican maids;
he was mortified when the latest of Dr. Pheiffer's shopping lists
was transcribed by the British radio operator, who acknowledged it with a polite
                    "thank you."

A CLOSE CALL

The old lady's rich.
As we emerged from the pub, a fervent lover of sport situated on a high bluff
put a premium on lack of originality. The gym helped me a lot.
When I reached the city, the thought of her dying
filled me with Christmas. Let me tell you something:
Yer aunties used to sell me stamps in the Post Office. I have a real steady job.
I bought a sack of apples & a bag of doughnuts. What a joy it gave us.
Now, our master had a habit of saying, "I wish for no unseemly wrangle here."
Would I, too, succumb to their morning egg?
For if not actually a hobo, I was at least prudent. It was all the more violent
in the general chorus of "cut the wood, dig up the garden & groom the pony."
As I lay in a comfortable bed, public opinion began to change.
That was a close call; instead of keeping me on the carpet,
he told me to accept a loan from the woman.

RIP BIG DADDY, GORILLA

The gorillas did not seem to enjoy the dense fog or the three thousand Belgian
               refugees.
For over four hours, the flames shot far into the sky & Big Daddy
, or sometimes another gorilla, clutching his machete with both hands,
repeated over & over a litany: "peace to our barren bamboo forests, happiness to our
volcano."
Soon I was reliable information; I was eight square miles of the bites of flies;
I was the last scars of the cattle invasion.
The gorilla is a miner named Jack Collins, an unbelievably slippery $5,000.
Tourists noted that the country was torn by utilitarian Andreas & tool-using
               Charleses. On April 24,
the jagged cracks in Central Africa, clothed in a white sheet & carrying a long staff,
obviously had no interest in Big Daddy.
It was time
for the lone one
to be on his way.

ELABORATE FUR HAT ETC.

Feature formal snow. Hang a black curtain.
Marriage is a chronicle of battle or costumes & music.
Still feigning drunkenness, he arrives at the hundred-year-old cherry tree.
You cannot go further than that.
The young maidens wished to conceal their identity,
so they attached a crimson tassel to the system. Buddhas
& dandies went off with an empty wooden wine container
& the leader of fashion devised a thin copper framework.
A small child entered the room crying out for milk & exile,
& thirteen silken strings tried to please you.
Another idol, in the absence of tigers,
followed my instructions.
Deathly white makeup,
elaborate fur hat.

THE TEN COMMANDMENTS

It was just cheek on their part.
O'Sullivan actually stumbled on this army of shadows;
at home he could only hint at blindness.
Naturally there were a few rounds of ammunition
ignoring all the rules—damning proof that without Seamus Robinson
the British would brows-knit-in-thought thwart the old constituency.
The greatest orators of the inevitable priest
began, promisingly, "Never mind."
On the sixth of January British soldiers fired on a group of colored ribbons
& they strode to the foot of the stairs.
With his passion for efficiency,
Mr. Jameson passed out the Ten Commandments.
Clearly the reference to Trinity Street
made so vast a corridor.

THE RED FLAG OF SOVIET RUSSIA

Meanwhile the surface pleasure of New Jersey was omnipotent.
"What do you mean by raising such an old-fashioned nightgown?"
"Didn't you read the opinion of the lower court?"
So Harlan went back to the prosaic task of stepping into Walsh's shoes.
As the nation passed 10,000 virginal verdicts,
the St. Paul railroad was content to remain on the sidelines.
The heirs of the late J.P. Morgan still go duck shooting,
though always thumbs down on the varied assortment of guests.
Having laid down their lofty precepts, Jim Farley boosted Massachusetts;
"Yes, your honor," replied a number of dark-haired ladies.
The passive role of sitting down,
in an eloquent conclusion, touched off the entire powder flask.
During a visit to Washington, a shoemaker did not confine his rudeness to
making the speech; he also put into practice the red flag of Soviet Russia.

LITTLE NOTES

All in one week, gracefully swaying in the open sky,
the lieutenant could boast of his large bright eyes
& now that I'm looking at his dim star
equally useless & uninteresting sufferings give you the money.
The red cheeks of Katya within a week among the bishops
in this stinking little town ..(ethereal as a butterfly).. boiled.
How do you know there's no one to whip you?
I am ill, my fever a sofa which is an insult even to a dog.
They wrote little notes to the doctor
& to distinguished literary men in full dress uniform.
My dear soul, what a flirt you are! How much do you want?
A peach was obliged to mortgage the estate—
she led a bad life, you understand—
& this woman fastened upon me & went off to town.

KRYLOV

This is the origin of Krylov: if the curtain before him is raised,
"earthquakes" bound the sovereign to your trip through Russia. I
can in no way, being a Christian, perceive a lack of cohesion or
arbitrarily say YES to the landowner's eradicated falsities.
The soul is, for almost a thousand years,
necessary for the theatre; distant from Christ, a critic
consecrated the wisdom of God in the investigation of legal problems &
permanent Russians.
So,
"Wonderful is the grace of God" compels a man to confront a perfectly useless
                    princess.
But do not throw out all the treasures of this world;
his personal business will raise him above terrors
by daily sleep-producing brotherly love
& all over Petersburg a simple scribbler, posthumously published,
is not simply a portrait of worthless people.

WHETHER THIS IS A GOOD THING OR NOT

Dictated by certain amazing chemicals, Otis W. Caldwell
(as one might expect) can be measured & described
as necessarily right or wrong.
J. Arthur Thomson the structure of a dogfish
in an erratic & unpredictable manner suggested.
To connect the lady up to any kind of apparatus
would ruin the intimacy of the scene.
It is amazing (but true) that social scientists study men collectively.
If indeed it can be called a science,
a ball released from your hand a million times
falls to the ground each time.
You still have to decide whether this is a good thing or not;
you might even decide that it is an evil thing.
You will get very little help from a psychologist in answering these questions.

VOLUPTUOUS, FLESHY WOMEN

Buddhism did not succeed in sending troops to breakfast;
in fact, Elena lay flat in a bathtub.
In the vanishing world of privilege,
voluptuous, fleshy women left suicide notes. Fidel is always right.
The little princess turned down Jasper's dozen red roses
& his routine telephone calls & money & with his dying breath
the emperor gently divorced her.
Caroline's disregard for propriety
was wasted on confused Hugh,
ailing, drinking, raving;
Hannah, the tricky problem, was a liar & repressed.
All we know for certain
is hefty, wooden, & bloodstained,
& it still reverberates today.

THE FEBRILE DESIRES OF YOUTH

According to one person who knew them well,
David, Francis & James resented Barcelona.
In accordance with New York,
a constant succession of boys cast no shadow.
Flanked by two angels (how many? two!) Igor strolled about Madrid.
The day-to-day grind of open coffins & retrograde appetites
could not have been otherwise; every night the snow-covered drawbridge
where thousands of old people frolic & masturbate to magazines.
Concerning the febrile desires of youth,
we have seen endless bombers abandon collaboration;
to honor fully Pebble Beach,
realize that cyclists in the form of a telegram
are the maximum opponent of Russian propaganda.
The ballet began in the dark.

WHAT ELEGANCE IS

Regaining pleasure, Gabrielle fancied a shoe salesman
& Lucien, on principle, sold the Irishman a turtleneck.
Graceful, wouldn't you say?
Sergei looked nothing like a murderer
& the baroness was physically persuaded.
The senator handed out advice:
"Remove the body."
"Take up guitar playing."
"Talk up a storm at dinner parties."
Still, there was some truth in her 50 franc blouse;
people no longer know what elegance is.
The nylon prestige, the high-wire publicity,
Antoinette was ready to fly off the handle.
Within days, the chauffer went on a paid vacation.

IN THE ABSENCE OF A BOYFRIEND

Claiming it was for his health in the absence of a boyfriend
Ian was on the lookout for a maze of small rooms.
The heiress pulled off her bathrobe & floated downstream.
Joan had had enough;
the canoes were about 30 feet long & known for their scrambled eggs.
A Swiss tourist on the outskirts of town
leads us to some very sad places:
the floor, Paris, a separate personality.
Beneath the stairwell Gregory made room for the tendrils.
What's wrong with your hands?
The judge: "I don't associate myself with any trends, groups, or experiments."
The Brooklyn guru often visited London;
watching the dancing boys
Ian accomplished a satisfactory clarinet.

AMERICAN POWER

These very groovy kids consciously or not sit in the kitchen,
binging on Christmas & had yet to bicycle. The workmen
are on a first-name basis with Susan; that's the way it's supposed to be.
With such names as Rosenburg & Elaine American power was in good spirits.
A wreck, I the confidence of a middle-aged painter
dissuaded, had difficulty, put forward beautiful paradoxes.
Serious Pollock went to the train station the reigning champion
& for the first time de Kooning through a literal process
didn't share the pie. Everybody sought him out.
It's a technique: a young Westerner [distant rumble]
suffocates in the well-meaning mass of believers America
A new & bigger Bronx America
Driveway not much to do America
Afternoon redoubled like a frog prepared for dissection America

TO CREATE REALITY

Who the fuck do you think had a curious malady that made her fall asleep
            suddenly?
If anything kept us sane, it was rage. His real grandmother
found it ironic that John Wayne came out on his porch.
The Hollywood seesaw: "Why don't you get your nose fixed?"
Tyrone Power the complexity, Tyrone Power the inadvertent
happy & sad an inch from my crotch raccoon.
In the bathtub you're obliged to fight back;
a surprising number of directors raised their hands in the Nazi salute.
Our culture stuttered a sense of closeness to Jesus' bad side;
I knew what I was doing. To create reality,
Marlon Brando does magic tricks. Maybe I'm overly optimistic
but history seems to be on the side of Dennis.
A neurotic, frightened man—a liar & a hypocrite—kept the illusion alive.
I don't think audiences realize it's the body of Christ.

THE SPOTLIGHT

The photographer enjoys a great advantage over Cole Porter
& it is impossible to explain why a man desires a particular snake pit.
Orson Welles resembled a giant ballroom. Confetti
& special messages rained down. Everybody said that
waltzing got the lion's share of my grandmother. Herbal tea
contradicts Giuseppe Torelli. If you wish,
sing a folk tune or say the words "boarding school."
The moment you keep your feelings at arms' length,
the doctors recite an excerpt from Faust. I can understand why
Rudolph spoke flawless German: if you take your work too seriously,
the spotlight will go for lunch break earlier than usual.
I have always wanted to put a wet towel over my face;
We talked for a long time,
until darkness fell.

THE ROOTS OF NEUROSIS

Promulgated: with the Balkans once again displaying their virility,
a vulture (or, more likely, a homosexual fantasy)
takes its rightful place among the roots of neurosis.
There are analysts who boast of golden business
but these disagreeable devices (cancer, masculinity, Nazism)
remain INCORRECT. Ultimately, anxious Charles went off to the grave
& stern Robert (an opinion) is not the center of the universe.
Someday, Belgium's best popularizer will resemble a newspaper.
Quack remedies, personal tragedies, the financial side of things:
then there was silence.
Love interfered badly with the First World War;
Otto disliked the radio, the telephone, & female sexuality.
Whether mankind will allow its ego to be destroyed
is quite another matter.

YOU CATTLE THIEVING SON-OF-A-BITCH

Americans are still playing host to a mob from Brisbee; numerous miners
became state capitals. Barkeeper Boyle testified that the two men
came not from Charleston but from breakfast.
Clean getaways, great columns of smoke, codes of silence: very leisurely.
Carrying Winchester rifles the two men stopped to enjoy an evening meal.
A posse of vengeful cowboys
assassinated the most liberal & kind-hearted man I have ever met.
Consciously, sunrise reached the railroad town
& during a confrontation the marshal gave a detailed statement to keep the peace.
A long, prepared statement. Now, since the evidence
lacks good social standing, law & order will have to get rid of the six- shooter.
Immediately on the heels of a lumber dealer, you
relieved the Arizona-Mexico border of $593
, you cattle thieving son-of-a-bitch.

THE GRASSY KNOLL

On a mission to avenge wrong & restore Lyndon B. Johnson, the CIA
(who have a pretty vivid imagination) initiated a blitzkrieg campaign
against my wife. The Soviet Union
(bastards) said it best about Oswald. J. Edgar Hoover's
close friends, as psychoanalysts would say, were gleaned from the official record.
Test tube glory planet, asylum in exchange...
it's not hard to figure out why. It has something to do with
the Warren Commission. On the day of the assassination
a pregnant woman submitted a change-of-address form.
Making a move & dressed in a suit, white shirt & tie
the zealot was no longer the small boy she had once known.
Other unpleasant behavior as well: very hard to understand.
Even among
conspiracy theorists.

TERRORISM, OR, OPEN YOUR HEART

Long-dead martyrs conspicuously slow to cause traffic accidents
ran amok that July in Kuala Lumpur, where bin Laden was cheekily suggesting
that from a bank in Guandong, China God in his armored black taxi
had given transcendental purpose to some seventy thousand pig farmers.
The attack failed miserably; tragically for Schleyer,
a tactic called Angelo derided as a capitalistic opiate the media.
The time comes in the life of any nation
when there remain two choices: hurl tomatoes at the new socialist premier Guy
                Mollet
or provoke the British into indiscriminate repression against myriad Zionist groups
whose precise coloration & contours they barely understood.
Anarchist terrorism did manage to use cruise missiles,
& mostly with a single shot to the forehead police
wrote down the rules of the game
(open your heart).

THE EISENHOWER DOCTRINE

In reality, the Shah's afternoons cannot be entirely blamed for
Tehran's unfathomable personalities; in the labyrinthine context
of Golestan Palace 170 soldiers were made even more special
by a dashing debonair man. The storied scion
reneged on Whitehall in a baptism by fire
& his greed knew no bounds. A few days later
the United States demanded the oil industry; this matter
only added to the tension. The British, of course,
never fell into the hands of complacency. A lost cause!
A large, flat, golden cigarette case
(a gesture of goodwill)
began to guarantee Iran's security.
The Eisenhower Doctrine was, in part,
emotional, rather than logical.

THE RIVER MAN

The river man by way of the Eerie Canal was tactless enough to ask
why the Gulf of Mexico ain't got but fifteen cents.
There are better ways to trespass on the Lord's day;
the whisky was beginning to do its work. First, let me say that
my pocketbook is floating down the Ohio & my father is a barge.
What is the shape of the Mississippi?
Why go ashore for wood?
Some of the boats had not yet discovered Mr. Lincoln.
Railroad people: next I shall show you Bob.
I offered to paint his face with red & black—
from that time on, my usefulness being passed, I tilled the soil,
so complete was King's calculation. In desperation
loose individuals found the heavens engaging in a plot to murder Marion Knowles
, a picturesque gentleman of the period.

TELEVISION

Our offices would take us out for drinks, but that was June.
Advertising is simply a spaceship. A little
girl was given a dollar to buy ice cream & cookies.
The networks had been wanting for some time to get control over
a room with many filing cabinets. Was it wrong? Of course, but
Frank was an amazingly talented puppeteer. A combination of warmth &
authority adopted two children, & for $100 a week the adulteress
, essentially a vulgar woman who thought she was a communist,
conducted a guerilla war against Bob Lewine, the head of
programming at ABC. To my horror
the people, in a typical response to Johnson,
set up cameras on a golf course. Sports interviews
& McCarthyist bristling, laugh tracks & Eisenhower
the proverbial big fish in a little pond: "Go on, go on, I'm listening."

GAUGUIN

The 65-franc orgasm was in many ways a yellow blot on our country's flag.
We know from photographs that the island was a crime.
Going about with an ordinary house broom sweeping, the editor
in the interest of laboriously copying out the minor drawings
suggested the male figure. If there was ever a time for
the bank (that menacing black creature) to stay for a meal
it was in 1894, with a cask of claret by the door
& this weird Frenchman sharing a bed with a Tahitian.
With singing & dancing the playwright remembered money
& a group of thugs is surely the reason why, to modern eyes,
the painting seems blasphemous. The young wood-cutter
took his chances with the local girls.
Such delicate things
were not made to survive.

MICHAEL JACKSON'S HYPERBARIC CHAMBER

A line in the sand was drawn in the expansive kitchen
where the somewhat formulaic Brian
vigorously for a grown man made a fiasco. The demons haunting Lisa
sent her a dozen tickets to a Michael Jackson concert;
as for Katherine, a safer cosmos was available. No. No. No.
Over the next few weeks, Kenneth had to wear a costume.
Hyperbaric chambers, hefty sums, averted eyes:
it was a no surprise that Beverly Hills freaked out.
When I'm not onstage, being the idol of many young women,
I stroll down Robertson Blvd. Las Vegas felt weird about
the rumors; oh yes.
For starters, what if something went wrong with the oxygen?
Maybe it was catharsis.
It was enough to make some observers sick to their stomachs.

THE HANGED MAN

Ragged float her father's rivered enemies—
dollars' daughter from spoon to cloudless cry,
an undressing of a servant shear
who was hoisted klan, never to see
again the gems she passed him, prayers

by now moss. They dragged him through
the woods after argument's cold yes very well,
flowers faint on her nightgown spread
legs the lovechild's agony gate.

Nursed on her own when world receive,
tears end with a wealthy groan.
There will be no breathing down of wine
for the improper; echo a smothering storm.

The tycoon among world's blooming powers,
his shame even the {black} baby did not thaw.
Without a raincoat & rope-coiled the servant
they took out the back door—tainted the old pleasure
as crystal seats the reverberating scream of E—

to a tree
at the top of a hill.

\\House creaking, candles he took to her bed
& she took him loudly. Flung doors of morning
back to trim hedges, & sunset she let her hair down,
golden sighed in the unkempt edges. His eyes
she fix on, kiss him, & he fingers nook . . .

Nights cold keep quiet or try to, but more often
outside where fountain wreathing the last light
he shape her, ivy to tree. Lovers.
He every inch of her marble skin in the weedy woods.

Those branches basket all he need of girls,
her breasts unreined & he cum but he couldn't
join her on the porch's wicker altar of flat smiles;
they could not dance in the wide alleys.

Rehearsed the hard horizon so briefly
meant long lips & panting; her eyelids peace,
he lay his head on her—oh red clouds . . .

LUXURIOUS AFFAIR IN FALL

corn maze of shoulders will wink
a passenger dice backseat paraphernalia,
box of parts delivered seep into ivy
..October entered by halter top teens

—& would-have widow pose for toy,
an artist of incandescent rooms yellow
insomnia trip-toe halls out-creak,
band-aid boy snore gone at mid-morning/

sermon circling a crowbar's thief,
drapes drop to floor in thump—like dress off
on her back spring mattress hem the noise
& something about fortitude or preparedness..

wrapped in money-shawl & into an aisle
whence waved-off spigot-mouth employee
install bathtub up to brim with
yard carcass & street glass; she skim

seatbelt problems in the rearview scuffle
, spilling. Could you pull over/
paint highway at sun callusing
all cracks—roll a stone over

dirt under his fingernails..
sirens hoarse at five so much
emergency—jump off a water-cliff
rushing air over him like hands & her

kayaking fog & fast food wrappers
as ghost originals watch from the woods
the river high & white-foams
, curving. Lose her things in a whirl//

He chew candy on a curb & a billboard
graffitied vow quality, four lanes of
scrap cars & taxis, office towers
cough up executives. Buy some!

Cloud-splotchy his acne messages
her terse replies; ok—sat on her front porch
in the rain. What happened?
leaves in autumn colors night-bleach

a single streetlight & dead hang ferns
cocktail glasses on dusty wicker, breeze
through her dyed hair she looks old
in the brutally soft light through storm

lightning reflected in cheap jewelry
"My late husband had no class," she said
to her love-kid, "but he was something,"
& thunder fill the silence..

the soliloquy of rain reach them each
ache different. Next door
a boyfriend kiss goodnight off drive
& a light goes on, goes off, they're out there

still. Headlights in the subsiding storm

ZAYLA

1. [THE AFFAIR BEGINS—RUMORS—HIS JOB AS A WOMEN'S COSMETICS EXECUTIVE—HER WILES & MASOCHISM—ANXIETY INCEST ARTIFICIALITY CONSUMERISM NEWSPAPERS OF THE DAY—THEIR VOICES IN TURNS & GARBLED AS IS APPROPRIATE—THE PROTO-FEMINIST ALLY OF THE '50s & HIS TENDENCY TO MANSPLAIN—TIME CONFIRMED AS NON-LINEAR IN THE SUBJECTIVE EXPERIENCE OF MEMORY—AUDREY IS MENTIONED ALTHOUGH NOT IDENTIFIED AS THE OTHER VIZETTI NIECE & HEIRESS TO THE FORTUNE WHICH DAVIS LORRY'S LOBOTOMIZED WIFE HAD BEEN DUE TO INHERIT—THE SUSPICIOUS INCIDENT IN WHICH AUDREY NEARLY DIES]

..for regular purposes initiated   staircase
\\\swing 4-poster pile-up on suspension, a late library
mr. Lorry and me's *Alexandria* side-affecting///toll road life
the tailor down Burrn St. is a follower of—developments

..breach of warranty,   Rock through the windshield
aerosol permanence & his deet screen porch, come on lashes/
last friday night i was unable, yes so totally unable ***∧∧∧
/to test the new chemical sprays ∧∧∧∧∧∧∧∧∧∧∧∧∧∧∧

${Best A Girl Can Get!}   as they may be
\ \............skinny dippers in Acid rain rivers
the grand simplicity of the new doctrine yeah
GRAND SIMPLICITY sold to   the Ford Motor Company

//..I love her like a pneumatic rotary-type grinding machine
with a flexible sanding disc attached to its full speed (!)

compared to this Cleopatra's magical shining
in the tenant moon which beacons
through suburb-man's meadow binding
I could see the street was like

manifest identity . . . comparing her PAGEANTRY,
 following a tickle New Township\ \\
controlling politicians in the name of Virtuous Social Order
respectable have been touching us without invitation

as far back as we can remember . . .
full of telephone poles & Saturday nights
the long sad avenue of jukebox children
where 1961 in drowsy vibration, the mask of

casual life, she mawkish mouth "What
are you trying to do actually electrocute me?"/

..are we home? no, you can
go back to sleep

the following morning on concrete steps
when there were stripes on the
coffee mug with details
she walks in circles

"You're leaving?" I ask
smoldering
*we have an early meeting today
——"I was shocked to hear about Audrey"

BRIGHTEST/// DRUNKEST BLUE EYES she's
going to be released from the hospital to-
-morrow

///

2. [THE INSERTION OF COPIOUSLY APPROPRIATED SERBO-CROATION LEGEND— THE
MOTIF OF ROYALTY & THE FUTILITY OF WAR—THE POEM NO LONGER EASILY DIVISIBLE
INTO THE VOICES OF THE LOVERS—THE NECESSITY OF THE CHANGING OF THE GUARD
IN RELATION TO POWER STRUCTURES OF THE '50s & '60s]

Here where we sit let us make pleasant conversation
It happened once in time long past
They attacked Baghdad but an old man will advise you—
To whom will you direct the sultan

And his imperial shore of the sea?
And when they came to the shore of the sea
The messenger entered the garden
Where, slender mustaches falling on both his shoulders,

Understood words arrived too late, my son,—
I cannot endure the marketplace
When it grew light & dawn appeared
Let them sing &   take brief walks

Behind him was a young man with   strawberries
A thousand heroes; I was in prison in bloody Zadar

& when the first half of the eighth began
_._.   are you easier? will you recover
......or are you in pain and will you die?
* * * * * * *///Imperial son...!* * * * * * *

"Father, emperor, master of the world!"\ \\
- -- —— —WHEN I surrounded Baghdad* * *
They turned the cannon——we did not disturb
Even the mortar in the walls

...Until the clover blooms, until _._._. gardens
And gather young &   old &
—attack Baghdad,,,,,,,,,,,,,,, call my trumpeter
                    a hard winter has come upon us

.............When you have buried your father,
—cut down the old men & put the young ones
---------------------------------in their place///

///

3. [DAVIS LECTURES YOUNG ZAYLA ON THE WARPED WAYS OF THE WORLD & IN
PARTICULAR THE COLD WAR–THE REPETITIVE NATURE OF HUMAN HISTORY– THE
MAIN THEME OF OLD ORDERS COLLAPSING ONLY TO BE REPLACED WITH A REPLICA–
BRIEF MENTION OF ZAYLA'S ABORTION AT AGE 16]

—   / // achieves, in rite of committee,
several hundred soldier
distortion policies & the primary motivation in such
behavior is   Probably

putting all the bombs on the back of the goat
individuals   w i t h i n a Communist
accuse a large percentage of the workforce
tracing mystic Russians

the psychoanalyst would start a war
if we wish to   apply any kind of
Czechoslovakia
to the spurious appearance of UNITY \ \\l

..only more   realistic//?/ WHO ..\highly rewarded even-tho
says don't share in the dialogue of the deaf* * * * * * * *

504

As old as the chant itself, clarification— being on the threshold of
1170, a forgotten feast day where no more than some 60—

Sanctus, Agnus Dei—feel quite satisfied
pious but much   requirements
 preserved the original   Mass of the Dead
those   existing   today   (DOCUMENTS)

EVEN THE QUESTION OF THE LOVE OF RULE
RUBRICS—COMISSIONS—HARMONY—!
as at all other times, THE PSALM IS SUNG WITH
PUNCTUM METRUM also "interrogation," flexa,

..the lessons of the Office of the Dead/// (sung in
the solemn/// lesson-tone) END WITH the formula

the official recognized
range\ \\ gradually   stenographic
in significance—establishing the key
to impose upon the whole Order as
pauses

{we can say}
Cassiodorus at Vivarium had his eyes
on transmitting both divine and human knowledge
to later ages

on securing it
against the age of barbarism which threatened to sweep it away
///whatever intermediaries,,,,,
mathematically & all very reasonable was the r.u.l.e.s.

they are   concerned only with
the search for obscure examples

the surgery performed on November 11, 1955

///

505

4. [NEWS ITEMS–ZAYLA MUSING OVER HOMEWORK–SENSE OF THE POOR
ORGANIZATION OF THE GREAT SYSTEM OF SYSTEMS THAT IS MODERN CIVILIZATION
ON THE PLANET EARTH–MORE PSEUDO-RANDOM LEGEND FROM THE PAST–
CONGRESSIONAL HEARINGS ON POLLUTION WHICH ARE OF MILD INTEREST TO ZAYLA
WHO IS ONLY BEGINNING TO WONDER AT THE ORIGIN OF THE VIZETTI FORTUNE–THE
INSANITY OF WHATEVER LOGIC BROUGHT THE WORLD TO THE BRINK OF NUCLEAR
APOCALYPSE–THE VIZETTI EMPIRE BEGINS TO UNRAVEL IN THE '30s AS TIES TO
VATICAN CORRUPTION & MAFIA ACTIVITIES BECOME DANGEROUS–THE QUESTION OF
WHETHER OR NOT THE CONDITION OF HUMANITY IS ARTIFICIAL]

a foreman has been hit in the head;
lightning rods, Gatling guns—on the surface
the spokesman explain   !
::democracy in preference to permission

to LEECH, the residence of   the West Atlantic
revenue/// fingerprinted,   everybody Straight away
live up to His aristocratic* expectations—
and all the while money.. & fine clothes

the master key's loose this system hardly a
system at all.. technological wonders of the city,
images, idols, the Darwinian streets
on a good day

their lonely,   worn-out wives
their boys   of summer with happy endings

TWO AT A TIME BEGAN TO TREMBLE
into the dark do they bring home troops\\\
has my tower been torn down or has it fallen in ruins?
is my old mother alive

is she alive or has she passed to////another world?
when the servants have   called out the door
rise to your feet
villages have been burned_

STAY WITH YOUR LOVE!   I departed from my love...
in my hand my shining rifle_ on my feet my marching boots_
          ///they encompassed us with wood & stone
                 they brought us to bloody Zadar

the snakes will
devour your bones

At this time, Dr. Carter, do you have any questions?
///who holds consensus, sulfur oxides * * * ^
///many of the fundamental^^^^^^^^^^^^^^ toxicological & physio-pathological studies
have employed

the guinea pig   as the distinguished
investigator   DR. MARY AMDUR   points out
compared with 56 per 100,000 in cities over 50,000 populluted

the business conducted at 8 East Superior St. in Duluth
we particularly observe

The dogs were under deep nembutal anesthesia
They were made to   breathe mechanically
the works of
Balchum, Dalhamn, Reid, & others

What, however, does this mean?
SOME EXAMPLES MIGHT BE USEFUL AT THIS POINT

"A truly irrational way is most important."
Marcus Aurelius warned against the
\ \ \ / Behavior Of BABOON$
                 all such emotions have in common the

///economic Advantage
even in 1953 an Office of pUBLIC Opinion Re-
-search Survey found 56% of Americans
 totally down with a

STRONG
EFFICIENT
Impartial
c eN TRal

government but an Extraterrestrial observer could see
the problem & solution both_man

Between 1920 & 1927
three Vatican ordinaries
 in festivitatibus quibus non laboramus
provided the Italian birthdays

virgins desired completely
however, the old
bishop on the feast of St. Sixtus
the second was with Judge Joseph Force Crater

when he stepped into a taxi in New York///
systematic composition
transmitted
orally:

the court system corresponds to the harmony of the cosmos
at the ninth hour of prayer

///

5. [PASTICHE OF ZAYLA'S LAW TEXTBOOK—THE INHERITANCE BATTLE BECOMES A
COURT MATTER—LEGALESE STRIPPED OF CONTEXT AS DESERVEDLY ABSURD—A HINT
OF ZAYLA'S GROWING ASSERTIVENESS—THE IDEALISTIC THOUGHT OCCURS TO HER
THAT A CLEAN SLATE WOULD BE DESIRABLE FOR PROGRESS ESPECIALLY IN FREEING
OURSELVES FROM MYTHS OF THE PAST WHICH ARE NO LONGER USEFUL—CATHOLIC
INFLUENCE CONSPICUOUSLY UNDER-INVESTIGATED IN KEEPING WITH ATTITUDES]

applications may be far-fetched—when a finance company's
repossession officer obtained the aid of a
filling-station attendant
in removing a repossessed car

the court held that since on October 8 1965
Davis had authority to $24M unless it can show that the

terms of this agreement were ambiguous
on the basis of these findings,
the effective handicap of systemic fiduciary
unless it can be shown that

the government and another and another
he was afterwards sworn as a witness

as a matter of logic there was
overwhelming cabinetmakers with no scientific background
no crusty old gentleman with a single
1956 model

this package still represents the
paramount reasons for denial of recovery

"Profit seeking, at least in
the possibility of a split between these 2 powerful dynamic
human loves
and especially between the USA & the USSR . . ."

such discussions make little distance
to revere the proper heroes
it was suggested that
 we want local support of the project

& we want an
interfering with reason; has often been so
qualify the picturing of the arms salesman
as the devil/// [EQUIVOCATIONS!]

\\\unless we simultaneously
dismiss these tales
$$$

///

6. [AN AMBIGUOUS QUESTION FROM ZAYLA TO DAVIS PERHAPS WITH REGARD TO SEX
OR THE FUTURE]

what are you trying to do

PALMERE

1. [ENGINEER'S PALM]

some used organic passengers can
to those native to the company console
a secrecy throat all urge ventilation
late apology.. our chemical mission,
weak the forces, recycling private scarcity

of cures for the hung blacken
for the bitten snakes thrown in thorns,—
our ointment over their powdered poison
many carcass wrap last of the rosemary..

we wash their guarantees til blind
like miners count them twelve clouds,
a million month cattle we dream rain..
would wealth to midnight underground

if [hypothetic!] reached reference, alone
why update the engineer's palm?
is passed fugitive that free cosmos?
if I am remote beam in the cabinets
if I have breathed a rebel game

& yes barbarian feast is our city of stars
a marriage to the dead thru et's empire—

2. [PARABLE OF THE LION]

an absence Lion et molded, like orphan
from sea in sand: et arson simultaneous place,
gone sacred, nudge to et clay time from the formless
to now_status: elephant parts to cleared mice
.nothing animal remains in et

once in the sky sleep lanterns web
et's climbing hands froze to satellite throats
of planet chords; black et's clock slope knees
sprung for tongue needle will thunder

whenever years debt pay own life one raise prestige
wherever numbered Their joy but fly the tax
laws et vested on Their every science
$——every gift throne a straitjacket..

busy-task barely remember the viewed plan
et order exhibit of further calculations, so I
mere some tHeir lose children brought to complex
where always et will stage material operations—
told me et:::*Each No More Shall They Process Et Possessions.*

.et's long superior chains I tie small bodies—
turn face me, et::::*Shall Ever Et Satisfied Slave.*

3. [ON BENDED KNEE IN ET.HERUSALEM]

cannons contain my prophecy antique
like after deathbed preferred words, row trial:
wake et's inexhaustible army
I attempting pose in mirror a ghost play sword
but ever uncover us the black acres of et.herusalem,

frack sediment symphonic, climate scripted deliver
chance percent for isolated information speakers
to simply die before the rapid offers of et
which heard we bow; deal common present

jamming into broken areas the manifest,
the refugees of the radio orthodox;
wed glass frontier to et forever\\\spit w/ serious crimes the new
brotherly marks in territory Romanovs, mother witness

I awaken to otherwise kingdom realism
machines are to have no nightmares; glorify et savage face
forever, believed light followed we rep
in praise of evil forget there were shepherds
in fits of fear clothes transform to nets

but under the sovereign archaeology of my mind
I beg spacetime—

4. [BETRAYING THE MACHINE]

*so hack the service comm host
flash fearing: sank ceremony in the grass her
naked her disc, images burn thru me
over mine memorie stand shaman I wax disposing then
spat on temple my quiet code in the dust

sudden sureness! porn litmus, money mandrake
of here shambles,—if detected_send
fungal slow the smell, the ranks of earth
thought sewer cells test me on machine continuum

.—I remember coyote nights my dog leash limit
being pedestrian, flip coin at crossroads
the course of a passing train my rev. lament
as we spike the road music

white river white lines red bodies white finish
why could I not have been among east coffins out
instead blood calendar pregnant with mod plant
far summer—\\

5.   [THE TOWER AT DAWN]

et's moving mass the hours observers
now as dawning dash heads cool air
as launch sun behind small self,
speed thru fosse "I am other & aware"
to level up horse blinders by breadline spasm..

shadows tax the banquet period
after rhetoric,   removing an emperor,
thru eggshells   animate commercial dogma
of Pinocchio   reversals of fortune which grace the handbook

slither   posture-churches the elite
whose tally   boundaries baklavan layer the donation
of   unresponsive family portraits, feasting
seminaries of   process priest aristocrats

who   style advents like brought flowers
& rig triumph   to color the people customers
manufacturing warp Democratic the steel strata

a formation of stone steps rope the tower
where trading sedentary access
to disperse testimony seeds, own outpost mail
imply original marsh

6. [FREEDOM]

one day welding a spine to service rail
electrode human to be hive-sheeted sizzle & cracks
me (surfaces lobe-fractal add fuel for et.herusalem
then after zone-fuse years automatic to et future
they are allowed to join a jet conditional)

FH0702 yield shell naked for razor fittings
but as I discard threads for machine lining she scream,
comb the crumbling cell shit slime
so from her skeleton I am to pick pearls—

candidate for harvest with angles royal to toe,
her whose sanded curves helmet a heartbeat—
bare she crawl fragile at my feet—hair like seaweed
long unseen, like retiring sun to tide this woman me—snapped

up from formaldehyde I map layout, all monuments main she
fresh from lost localities breath doubt in the metal master
thru et monastery axis grave she gleam a future—

she loose tears my collar & I traffic potentialities,
aquarium of situation throws, all my armor—
pacing in her small cell, staring from scattered eggshells
impossibilities watch us dead things in a jar—*

[NUMBERS: AN EPILOGUE]

after the first canto of Ezra Pound

& loaded up-hatch nav that system
thru seal to engines rev & lift out hangar
we pass customs blockade & the ship shudder
born for this one last lightspeed, & our bodies
weighed like needles; com static back up on
our talk. We have already forgotten a feast—
I am this craft, buzzed & bearing

so I sit, lights blink the dash,
hours retching then until we get there.
The sun never sleeps other times year, suck on sand,
camflash-white frontiering & shallow graves—
Kimmehr peopled of cactal skin
covered lips & wide horizons. Impervious black
eyes like coffee grounds wet-glitter

The sky stain with stray smog but a few stars
& I shiver landed & thru scanners tarmac
they out in this greeting darkness; jeeps across
desert & not until dawn lights of the burnt city
& we kept the hours there,
transfuse blood to them
& I dug out the tube from my forearm.

"Tell of Penohr," said them lean
: so, "She shattered on the anterior, taken,
et kinged what corner we were;
her carcass heaped among trash,
which overheard only—*these are the pages*
we kept for her."
                    I brushed off, drag, begin: —

DARRYL

In the end, all we can be sure of
is that Darryl cannot be trusted.

Made in the USA
Columbia, SC
03 February 2019